Up From The Ashes

"40 Lessons of Faith
Towards Victorious Christian Living"

By

Andrew Bills

Up From The Ashes

"40 Lessons of Faith Towards Victorious Christian Living"

By

Andrew Bills

Copyright @ 2013
All Rights Reserved
Printed in the United States of America

By

ABM Publications
A division of Andrew Bills Ministries Inc.
PO Box 6811, Orange, CA 92863

www.abmpublications.com

ISBN: 978-1-93-182006-6

All scripture quotations, unless otherwise indicated are taken from the King James Version of the Bible, Public domain. Those marked NIV are from the New International Version, copyright @ 1973, 1978, 1984 by International Bible Society. Used by permission of Zondervan Publishing House. All rights reserved. Those marked NASB are from the New American Standard Bible, copyright @ 1975 by The Lockman Foundation and are used by permission. All rights reserved.

Special Dedication

To my loving wife,

Ann Marie

Thank you for your courage, faith, eternal love &
for trusting Christ and believing in my God given dream

Table of Contents

Forward

Special Acknowledgement

Introduction

1	How To Obtain The Favor Of God	1
2	How To Recover Joy After Experiencing Heartbreak & Sorrow	5
3	Are You Stressed Out Because Of Rebellious Or Screwed-Up People In Your Life?	7
4	Did You Know That You Cannot Run With The Turkeys If You Want To Soar With The Eagles?	11
5	Are You Sick & Tired Of Being Just Sick & Tired?	13
6	How Should You Handle Stinging Criticism, Ugly Comments and Negative Remarks From Others?	15
7	Are You Making The Most Out Of What You Have?	19
8	What Are The 3 Main Tools & Strategies Used Against Believers In Spiritual Warfare?	21
9	When God Is All You Have, You've Just Learned That He's All You Really Need	23
10	What's Holding You Back From Making Yourself Completely Available To God?	27

11	Did You Know That Experience Is A Teacher, But You Don't Have To Let It Become Your Undertaker?	31
12	Are You Still Living In The Rear View Mirror?	33
13	Why Do Some Find It Easier To Listen To Others Than To Take God At His Word?	35
14	Are You Afraid To Believe God Because Of The Opinions Of Others?	37
15	How Can We Be Sure That God Will Keep His Promises?	39
16	PRAYER – *That Makes Things Change!*	41
17	How Great Is Your Desire To See God Move In Your Life?	43
18	Are You Trusting The Lord Or Taking Matters Into Your Own Hands?	47
19	What Should You Do When "Goliath" Comes?	51
20	How Secret Are Your Secret Sins?	55
21	What Should You Do If God Seems Silent Or Absent?	57
22	Do You Have A Plan To Win Or Are You Just Trying To Survive The Day?	61
23	If Something Is Done In The Name Of Jesus, Does That Always Mean That Jesus Approves?	63

24	How Can I Overcome My Fears Through Faith In Jesus Christ?	67
25	Do You Want To Develop A Victorious Attitude?	71
26	Hurdles – How Should They Be Viewed?	73
27	Why Is It That Believers Often Fail To Pray?	75
28	Are You Aware That God Does Some Of His Greatest Work In The Midst Of Your Darkest Hour?	79
29	Are You Allowing Someone To Talk You Out Of What God Has Revealed To You?	81
30	Why Don't You Do Something That The Enemy Doesn't Expect You To Do?	85
31	How To Rebound From Defeat And Start Over After Disappointments?	89
32	Are You One Of The Lord's Heroes Of Faith?	91
33	Do You Find Yourself Doing Things You Feel The Need To Hide?	93
34	Is Seeing really Believing?	95
35	When The Thief Comes, Will He Find You Armed & Dangerous?	97
36	You Don't Drown By Falling Into The Water, You Drown By Staying There	99

37	Have You Experienced The Power And Healing Of Forgiveness Through Christ?	103
38	Are You Tuned In To The Voice Of The Holy Spirit?	105
39	How To Tell If You're Moved More By What You Physically See Or If You're Moved By Christ And The Power Of God	107
40	Show The Devil That You Don't Believe You're Defeated	111
	About The Author	115
	More Available Materials	117
	Ministry Contact Information	119

Forward

"A devotional is a spiritual thought or prayer that helps one gain an insight to who and what God is; It enables one to become more fervent, faithful and dedicated to a particular person or thing. It's one's private reach to the God he serves; It is man reaching Godward." NDR

As was said of David, Pastor Andrew Bills is truly a man after God's own heart. He labors to please Him in everything he does and believes in excellence, giving his best in every work or task.

His striving to do God's will has led him to help others reach out to God, knowing He is the answer to all of life's challenges. But many find it difficult to break through without being fed; for many are yet babes (1st Corinthians 3:1-2). They see the bottle but can't reach it or they need someone to put it to their mouth. Once done, they will freely drink and be filed.

Pastor Bills has taken the bottle of The Holy Word, mixed the formula in the right proportions so that the milk helps the little ones grow. Having read several of Pastor Bills' daily devotionals, I was very impressed with the beautifully deep yet simplistic presentation of material, which reaches the heart of the reader \hearer and touches his or her soul. His messages answer many questions as to how, why and when God will move in the life of an individual and what happens when an expected answer does come or doesn't come the way one may expect. You can tell from the devotionals that much prayer has gone into the preparation and God has visited the man.

In the 16th Chapter of St. John, the disciples adjure Jesus not to speak to them in parables any more, but to speak plainly to them. Pastor Bills must have heard the disciples' plea for his devotional messages are beautiful and plainly delivered.

Bishop Napoleon D. Rhodes

1st Prelate of The Convention of Covenanting Churches

Andrew Bills

Acknowledgements

"What is most needed today in this time of many bewildering troubles is good spiritual teaching. This is what the human heart is really hungering after. But not just any spiritual teaching will do. What is needed is an authentic spiritual teaching that is rooted in the Gospel of Christ and borne by an authentic relationship with the person of Jesus. This is what Pastor Andy Bills gives us in this book.

Practical and applicable teaching that has been tried and proven in the crucible of his own life. His writing is simple and direct but not simplistic. It is pastoral in style and profound in insight.

Pastor Bills displays the pastoral sense of the Apostle Paul as well as the wisdom of Solomon. Therefore I am pleased to commend this work of my friend and colleague, Pastor Andy, to both the beginner and the seasoned follower of Jesus."

Bishop Peter Elder Hickman

Presiding Bishop of The Ecumenical Catholic Communion

"Pastor Andy's reminders that we must actively seek God through our prayers and actions are a tremendous inspiration to me. Through his messages I am taught that I need to seek my answers from God and His words as recorded in the Bible and live the life in faith that God intends for me."

Gay Smith

Businesswoman

Andrew Bills

Introduction

"Up From The Ashes"

"I'm bringing you up from the ashes. Just like the 3 Hebrew Boys, I'm bringing you up from the ashes without any stench that you've ever been in the fire, through the flames or in the smoke."

This is a series of messages that **NO BELIEVER SHOULD BE WITHOUT!** It's here that you'll learn that **"the hardest spots in life can also become the places of new revelation or a new beginning in your life."**

Drawn out of the story from Daniel Chapter 3, these were the powerful and gracious prophetic words that were wonderfully spoken direct into my heart by The Holy Spirit of God many years ago as I was going through one of the most horrific, painful, challenging & devastating experiences that I've ever encountered.

Yet, I immediately perceived that this message wasn't only just for me but for the many others whose lives have been shipwrecked because of bad financial decisions, ungodly relationships, unforeseen or unexpected events, bad choices, abusive situations, chemical dependencies, painful conditions, loneliness, slander, divided homes, and even past hurtful church experiences.

Just like I discovered, you too should realize that the help you truly need will **NOT** come from moving to another community, finding a new love interest, watching TV talk shows and losing weight, making new friends, finding a new job position, winning the lottery, having another drink, smoking another cigarette or even eating another slice of pie, **"NO!"**

Arising from your wounded past will only come from fully embracing Christ, our Living Savior, placing your confidence in his Word and trusting him that by His Grace he will save, deliver, guide, heal, comfort, strengthen and provide for you as you turn to and fully walk in obedience to God.

Allow these messages to inspire and assist you towards having a joyous fellowship with The Living Christ and help bring you face to face with your divine opportunities from God.

THEREFORE, HAVE FAITH IN GOD!

Pastor Andrew Bills

Victory Fellowship Church of Orange, CA

and

"The Victory Report Hour"

**The Internet, Radio & TV
Global Outreaching Bible Teaching Ministry**

www.andrewbills.com

Up From The Ashes

"40 Lessons of Faith Towards Victorious Christian Living"

1

"How To Obtain The Favor Of God?"

Did you know that God can do more in one moment of favor than you could ever accomplish in a whole life time of hard labor without Him?

While we don't see an exact definition of it in scripture, there are 200 times where the word **"Favor"** is used throughout the Bible and many great examples are given of people who had **"the favor of God"** in their lives.

In each account, you'll discover that favor had **NOTHING** to do with good luck or wishful thinking. Favor is not some magic formula you must learn or recite or some secret ingredient pill you have to take. You'll also discover that it cannot be earned, purchased or achieved; it can only be **"RECEIVED."**

Next, it's important for people to understand and realize that God's Favor can find you wherever you are and in whatever situation or circumstance you may find yourself in. Unemployed, dealing with family problems, in financial ruin, sick, in a dead end job, lonely, out-numbered, living in an obscure environment, facing eviction or foreclosure, or even incarcerated.

There's **NO SITUATION** so dark or impossible that The Holy Spirit cannot enter into.

Well, what does **"Favor"** look like? How do we get it? Once we get it can we ever lose it? Is it only for a select or chosen few? Favor is God **"showing up and showing out"** in the life of any believer. You cannot force it, manipulate it or pretend that you have God's favor. Many false pretenders have come and gone, but Christ will always have the final say-so and render judgment.

God's favor is God divinely, supernaturally and graciously doing something that only He can do in your life for your good and His glory. It's God's Almighty hand at work in your life where only He can get the credit. **Its God doing for you what you cannot do for yourself or others in seemingly impossible or unfavorable situations.** Favor is His presence, grace and power wonderfully at work in your life to draw attention to Himself that He's mightily at work, orchestrating through you.

Now, obtaining the favor of God **DOES NOT** require a college education, a high credit score, any political connections or that you hold a certain religious position within your church community. **It is only received from God or bestowed upon anyone who has already dedicated, surrendered, committed, submitted, yielded, purposed in their heart or made a clear choice to take God at His Word and stand in faith against all the odds surrounding them that dictate otherwise.**

It's God then wanting to touch and bless your life to show the world who He is and what He can do for no other reason than to declare that **HE ALONE IS GOD AND THAT HIS WORD NEVER FAILS.** God's Favor in your life **does not mean** that you're now on **"easy street"** and that you'll have everything you want when you want it. Neither is God's Favor in your life just for your earthly convenience or to fulfill your fleshly desires. God's **"no genie in a bottle"** that if you rub you'll get 3 wishes that will make you happy.

God's Favor comes upon or dwells in the life of any believer that makes a clear decision to stand for God and believe His Word regardless of any contrary outward evidence, negative remarks, demonic activity, physical hardship, dark circumstances or impossible situations surrounding you. The Favor of God will be seen in any believer's life who demonstrates that obeying God is more precious to them than obtaining fame or fortune without Him. **It comes from denying your flesh because your love for Christ is greater than your love for the world.**

The favor of God was so upon the life of Noah because Noah believed in him when the rest of the world didn't. God then saved him, spared his family and delivered many of the animals from the worldwide destruction of the flood. (Read Genesis chapters 6-8)

The favor of God was so upon the life of Joseph that after proving that he believed God no matter what situation he found himself in, in one day God took him from the pit in the prison and set him at the right hand of the pharaoh of Egypt. (Read Genesis chapter 41)

Daniel purposed in his heart that he would not defile himself while in Babylonian captivity and God's Favor mightily moved upon his life in many amazing ways. (Read Daniel chapter 1)

Manasseh was the worst king in the history of Jerusalem. Murder, political corruption, bribery, human sacrifices, adultery, idolatry and greed had ravaged Judah, so God rose up the Assyrian enemy. They captured Manasseh, put a hook through his nose, led him like a common slave through the streets with brass chains on and then threw him in the Babylonian prison. **But, in 2nd Chronicles chapter 33, Manasseh repented, humbled himself, greatly sought the Lord and God heard his prayers.** God so mightily moved in his life that he was set free and then even brought back to the throne in Jerusalem as king of Judah. He then spent the remainder of his years undoing all the things he had previously done to bring honor to God.

Time here will not permit me to speak about the lives of others like Job, Enoch, Abraham, Moses, Gideon, Ruth, Samuel, David, Nehemiah, Esther, Mary the mother of Jesus, the Apostle Paul and so many others throughout biblical history that believed God despite the surrounding circumstances or impossible situations.

But, the Favor of God didn't end in Biblical times; it still wonderfully continues today. Will you let Christ reign in your heart? Will you permit God to place His hand upon your life? **Will you choose to stand up in a fallen down world for Jesus Christ?** Will you keep your mind renewed in The Word of

God? Will you allow The Holy Spirit of God to direct your path?

Secular history has revealed that God has mightily moved in the lives of farmers, factory workers, shoe salesmen, mothers and housewives, students, soldiers, truck drivers and the list goes on. **God is looking for anyone who will make this life-style commitment to Him.** Male or female, young or old, educated or unlearned, cultural background or denominational persuasion doesn't even matter to God. He's searching for those that He can spiritually, supernaturally and mightily operate in their lives and reveal Himself to the world through them. Will you say "**YES**" to the Lord?

2

"How To Recover Joy After Experiencing Heartbreak & Sorrow?"

While it may not seem easy to bounce back after your dreams have been shattered or your hopes have been crushed, **much depends upon your attitude and the confidence that you're willing to place in God and His Word as you go forward.**

In life we may not be able to choose what will happen to us but we are definitely in control of the attitude that we'll take when things occur.

So, you can choose to arise and continue or you can choose to stay down, drown in misery and suffer defeat, but know this: You have been given the power of choice and with God's help you can rise again if that's your desire and will.

Often, it may even take a little time to get healed and to start recovering your lost dreams or start having new ones, but, know this: It doesn't cost any more to dream big than it does to dream small, so why not dream big.

Yes, emotional pain resulting from negative experiences can have a devastating effect on you if you don't stop and do something about it today.

Such depression and inner turmoil affects your attitude and even changes your physical appearance as it takes you through mental anguish, emotional breakdown and even physical illness.

And Naomi was one who was experiencing this. She was so broken and altered by her painful circumstances that some who knew her best couldn't even believe their very eyes when they saw her.

She had become a shadow, a mere image or a poor figure of the woman that they had once known.

Ten years earlier she had left Bethlehem with her husband and two grown sons, but was now returning as a widow, childless, had sold the majority of her goods and personal effects and had nothing left but the very clothes on her back. **All she had was Ruth,** her loving and faithful daughter-in-law who, also being a widow, had vowed never to ever leave her side.

Now, Ruth 1:19-21 NIV says: *So the two women went on until they came to Bethlehem. When they arrived in Bethlehem, the whole town was stirred because of them, and the women exclaimed, "Can this be Naomi?" "Don't call me Naomi," she told them. "Call me Mara, because the Almighty has made my life very bitter. I went away full, but the Lord has brought me back empty. Why call me Naomi? The Lord has afflicted me, the Almighty has brought misfortune upon me."*

Naomi's heart-wrenching statement was in immediate response to those who were shocked, stunned and overwhelmed at the first sight of her appearance as she returned back.

Now, Please Listen Very Carefully! Satan will attack your mind as he will try to do all that he can to keep you feeling fearful, discouraged, doubtful, tired, stressed out, miserable, and weak.

Yes, and in doing so, you too will remain depressed, ineffective, confused, frustrated, mad, prayer-less, helpless, hopeless, useless, defeated, wandering around aimlessly and even angry at God.

Satan doesn't want you to become encouraged, inspired, strengthened, delivered, growing in faith, joyful, healed, having a vision, becoming blessed or receiving your victory from God.

Yes, Satan wants you to believe that you are beyond help and that all of the promises of God are for someone else, ***But, That's A Lie!***

Though your heartaches and sorrows were all planned by hell, your recovery, healing, deliverance, and victory are all organized and carried out by Heaven. So keep your face looking upwards towards the **"SON"** and let the dark shadows fall behind you.

Initially Naomi had returned back to Bethlehem with a broken heart, a drooping hung down head and a song of misery and defeat. **But, as she turned her face up to The Lord, God began to marvelously intervene in her life and in her affairs.**

Her eyes once again became elevated, hope was re-born in her heart and home, her needs began to be wonderfully met and Ruth began to obtain special grace and favor in the eyes, heart and mind of a wealthy devoted man, who believed God and married her. Then those that had earlier mocked and gossiped against them now began to hold her in high esteem, offering her praises, and blessed her. **(Read Ruth 4:13-17)**

And What God Did For Naomi And Ruth, He Can Definitely Do For You.

THEREFORE, HAVE FAITH IN GOD!

Andrew Bills

3

"Are You Stressed Out Because Of Rebellious Or Screwed-Up People In Your Life?"

"When you think that you're just about to win in this rat race, along comes more rats that are faster than you." Well stress, heartaches, mental anguish and emotional torment will wreak havoc and leave you shipwrecked..... *__IF YOU LET IT__!*

It doesn't matter if the person troubling, worrying or stressing you out is a family member or relative, a co-worker, a neighbor, a fellow student, a friend or even an ex-spouse. **The Bible has solutions on how to deal with rebellious or screwed-up people.**

Whether it's someone you love or a total stranger, our world is filled with people who will bring great anguish in your life because they think they're smarter than you, can do a better job than you, they're jealous of your position, envious of your talents, they're addicted to drugs, or they are just plain nuts.

Regardless if they're a **"pain in your heart or a pain in your butt,"** your starting point for obtaining victory or success despite them is through establishing and maintaining a clear vision of who you are in Christ, who Christ is in you and walking in His Authority.

Your situation is not unique. You don't have to allow others to put you through the wringer. You can learn how to overcome and even forgive without being trampled on when someone else is working overtime to cause you pain.

Just as a tragedy survivor has to come to grip with their new reality, you too must come to grip with yours in order to have vision and move forward. You either must make the choice to arise, be filled with a new vision and walk forward or to remain where you are and die. (And I personally don't recommend dying!)

We too must learn to answer every stressful temptation from rebellious people just like Nehemiah did in Nehemiah 6:3: "I am doing a great work and I cannot come down. Why should the work stop while I leave it and come down to you?"

Don't allow yourself to be overcome by any foolishness, no matter how urgent, repetitive or malicious. Know that you're in spiritual warfare and that Jesus said that **"the gates of hell cannot prevail against you."** (Matthew 16:18)

Nehemiah knew the spirit that he was dealing with from those challenging him and what they were aiming to do. While he didn't show any open contempt, he refused to relinquish his place, abdicate his God given position and stop doing what he was called to do.

Never step down to the level of your circumstances! Maintain your course of action. Keep a good conscience before The Lord and maintain a good reputation before whom you're called to witness.

Remember, whatever your anguish is the result of, you can learn how to stop, and then proceed by allowing God's Holy Spirit to quiet your soul and flood your mind with His peace through His Word.

Philippians 4: 6-7 says, "Do not be anxious about anything, but in everything, by prayer and petition, with thanksgiving, present your request to God. And the peace of God, which transcends all understanding, will guard your hearts and your minds in Christ Jesus."

The greatest source of power is God's Word, but you must connect into Him to be energized and turned on to receive your breakthrough, in the name of Jesus Christ.

THEREFORE, HAVE FAITH IN GOD!

4

"Did You Know That You Cannot Run With The Turkeys If You Want To Soar With The Eagles?"

Have you ever heard it said that, **"Birds of a feather, flock together?"** That's just a parabolic way of stating that the people and the things you associate with are either adding to your life or taking away from it because it's impossible not to imitate those that are influencing you from becoming just like them.

Achieving or wining is a continuing lifestyle that's filled with good choices and discipline. So, if you're unhappy with your lifestyle and you really want to change the direction of where you're going, one of the first steps is to carefully consider who you're **"hanging around with"** or what you're allowing into your spirit.

The people that you're associating with the most are the ones that are **"speaking into your life"** either by what they say or by what they do to influence you. They are either using you as a **"dumping ground"** for their negative and pessimistic comments, their critical and discouraging ways, their counteractive and ineffective ideas and their corrupt and deprave manners......

Or they're **"impacting your life, family, finances and your future"** through their constructive, spiritual, optimistic, positive, desirable, upbeat, faith-filled, acceptable and edifying ways, ideas, instructions, advice, assistance, guidance, wisdom and manners. Good role models are those people that refuse to accept their current conditions when they knew they were created for so much more.

God says in Proverbs 13:20 NIV, "He who walks with the wise grows wise, but a companion of fools suffers harm." Isn't it interesting **THAT IT'S NOT GOD** who will bring down the harm or destruction into your life, **NO,** it's following the advice, instructions, ways, influence, input and companionship of the foolish and unwise people. It will bring untold misery, depression and destruction upon your own head during this lifetime as well as for eternity.

Not only does it apply towards those you're associated or involved with but it also pertains to the type of television, radio, internet programming that you watch or listen to. The movies you see, the books, newspapers, magazines and other literature you read will also have a great impact on your life.

God is now saying that **"You Have A Choice Or The Decision Is Yours."** So, choose carefully whose advice you'll follow and what you'll be influenced by.

If a person gets out of prison, only to go back to his or her old environment, he has set himself up for re-incarceration. You must escape the environment in order to have a brand new beginning or fresh start.

You can overcome anything if you're first willing to be transformed. Learn to regulate and control your conduct and behavior by rising up, trusting The Lord and reaching higher.

So select your friends and associates carefully and be led by The Holy Spirit. Take on the mind-set of champions, the attitude of those who've achieved in the field that you're interested in and learn from their wisdom and commitment to excellence.

Develop the lifestyle of a winner simply by associating with those who are what you want to become. Learn from their character and re-shape your habits in order to become a high achiever and a good role model yourself.

Become a leader. Make prayerful and wise personal, career, family and financial decisions. Remember, **IT'S YOUR LIFE**, and it's just too precious to waste.

5

"Are You Sick & Tired Of Being Just Sick & Tired?"

Does it seem that everything is getting worse before it ever starts to get better? Well, you are not alone. **Then what are you to do in the middle of a stressed out situation?**

We are given a great insight from God in the story recorded in **1st Samuel 30:6 NASB. It says,** "Moreover David was greatly distressed because the people spoke of stoning him, for all the people were embittered, each one because of his sons and his daughters. But David strengthened himself in the LORD his God."

David and his 600 mighty men had gone off to war, leaving their village unprotected, and in their absence the Amalekites ravaged their homes, kidnapped their families and stole their cattle and belongings. Then upon their return and discovery, his troops overcome with grief, began to murmur and spoke of mutiny against him.

But, in the very midst of this horrific situation, David encouraged himself by turning directly to the Lord and set his face to seek direction and help from his maker.

He encouraged himself by getting before the presence of God, while standing on the promises of God and praised God for His faithfulness in keeping His Word. **He remembered his covenant relation to God,** and he remembered the grace, mercy, and the goodness of God throughout his past experiences. So, he fully hoped and believed that God would appear for him in some way or another, and once again work salvation for him.

David called for the Ephod, the priestly garments to be brought in front of his face, which signified the anointing and the presence of God. Then he sought the will of God, knowing that the person making an inquiry always placed the matter before God in prayer and then would receive an answer from God. **Shortly thereafter, David received a Word from The Lord that led to a full pursuit, recovery, victory and even greater blessings in their lives.**

We who live today, should open up The Word of God and cry out, **"Lord direct me in this matter in which I know not what to do,"** for He knows how to deliver the godly out of temptation, and how to handle every adverse circumstance, negative situation or painful condition that's ever before you.

Worshipping and believing God are the weapons of your warfare for **"attacking back,"** piercing through the darkness, breaking through any barriers, pulling down strongholds and overcoming all opposition.

Today, believers have the indwelling presence of The Holy Spirit and He's there to help you, so you must learn to tap into or extract down from Him by seeking God's face and trusting in the promises from our Lord Jesus Christ.

Listening to some good inspiring music, hearing some good gospel teaching and preaching, and then surrounding yourself with positive, spiritual and anointed influences always helps to breakout of any downward and negative mood swings, discouragement or depression and helps bring healing and inspiration to our souls.

As you meditate on Him and His Word and give Christ the praise, **He will always direct and lead you in the ways that you should go towards having blessed results.**

<u>**THEREFORE, HAVE FAITH IN GOD!**</u>

6

"How Should You Handle Stinging Criticism, Ugly Comments and Negative Remarks From Others?"

Isn't it simply amazing how people will rise up to criticize you when you start doing something for Jesus? **Well, how should you handle stinging criticism, ugly accusations, vicious slander, unkind comments and negative remarks when they come your way to discourage and attack?**

In the gospel of Luke 7:36-48, we are given the familiar story of Jesus and His disciples dining at the house of a Pharisee, called Simon the leper. During that feast, a woman carrying an alabaster jar of very expense perfume approached Him and after opening it, poured the perfume on Jesus' head and feet. Then, while weeping, she began wiping the perfume from His feet with her hair and kissed His feet in complete adoration of Him.

While the beautiful fragrance was wonderfully still in the air, many were troubled by this entire scene. Some challenged the waste of such an expensive perfume, scoffing that it could've been sold for a lot of money and given to the poor. But, during the very midst of vicious stares, gossip and even name calling, she didn't allow the shamefulness or embarrassment of being called **"a sinner"** discourage or detour her away.

The Pharisees began to condemn the fact that Jesus would allow such a vile creature and notorious sinner to do such a thing, let alone enter His presence. Many therefore concluded that since he didn't know her character and didn't rebuke her then he couldn't really be a true prophet. But, Jesus came into this world to seek and save the **LOST** and today, we must never forget our main mission is to continue to carry on as ambassadors for Christ.

This woman not only did what she felt led to do in her heart and soul, but did so in the very face of slanderous remarks and negative criticism. Where she had met Jesus earlier, or what message of His had brought life to her dead heart and soul, we are not aware of. **Her love for her Savior was greater than the slander of men.** Her humility poured from out from a heart that had been healed, forgiven and changed. Her dedication was so pure that she totally discounted the expense of her offering and the negativity of men. **Her only focus was on loving The Lord because the mercy and grace shown to her by Christ was far greater than the ugly comments from men.** What has Jesus done in your heart and life? What blessings has He done in your life or home? **Once you've counted His blessings, are you ready to pick up your cross and follow Him daily?**

In our world, criticism is something unavoidable and inevitable. And if you try to make everybody happy and love you, you're just wasting your time and energy. **While Satan will always try to use criticism to produce a stinging effect upon your mind, as a believer you must weigh it against the love, mercy, forgiveness, healing, deliverance and saving grace shown to you by our Lord.**

Often, the greatest stinging remarks or most negative comments Satan brings are from the mouths of those that are closest to you: family members, relatives or the closest friends. But, we must allow the peace of God to guard our hearts and not become distracted from our worship, fellowship with and service to God.

It's also very important to also understand that not all criticism is bad. We must have an open and discerning heart towards God's correction. **Constructive criticism will come from people who truly love The Lord, are filled with The Holy Spirit and desire to mentor you to grow.** Unfortunately, those who are **NOT** in love with Christ or sent by The Holy Spirit will only bring negative or destructive criticism. Don't allow their comments to bring you down, affect your relationship with God or prevent you from doing His will.

Jesus was so moved by her passionate and genuine act of devotion that He forever immortalized her by saying, "Wherever this gospel is preached in the whole world, what this woman has done will also be told as a memorial to her." (Mark 14:9) **And Christ today is still moved as we demonstrate passionate and genuine acts of devotion to Him** as we reach out to touch and impact the lives of others as we are led from a heart filled with love for Him.

7

"Are You Making The Most Out Of What You Have?"

Somewhere in all of our lives, we've had to say goodbye and bury a loved one. While walking through the cemetery one day, I observed several of the tombstones or grave plaques and noticed that they all had the same things: **a beginning date, an ending date and a hyphen or dash between them.**

The children you've raise, the college education you've received, the goals you've achieved, the money that you've made and all of the entertainment activities you've enjoyed **are all encased in the hyphen between those two dates.** Your life is a hyphen spaced between two dates, set between two divine appointments. While these two dates were set by God, **what's vitally important is how you fill in the blanks between your eternity past and eternity future.**

James 4:14 NIV says, "Yet you do not know what your life will be like tomorrow. You are just a vapor that appears for a little while and then vanishes away." **Then God says in 2nd Corinthians 5:10 NIV,** "For we must all appear before the judgment seat of Christ, that each one may receive what is due him for the things done while in the body, whether good or bad."

Some people measure life in years just like they would measure water in cups. But in the same sense, your cup of water compared to the Pacific Ocean is just like comparing your brief life to all eternity.

So, make the most of your life. Do the right things. Worship God, walk in fellowship with The Living Christ, learn to overcome set-backs, learn to smile and laugh, enjoy your family, and raise your children in the sight of the Lord.

Life's a one-way journey. **Again, make the most out of it, have faith in God and do what's pleasing in His sight.**

8

"What Are The 3 Main Tools & Strategies Used Against Believers In Spiritual Warfare?"

The way you live your life and conduct spiritual warfare reveals if you believe **"The Most High God or the most low devil."**

Winning battles doesn't require physical strength, a multitude of people behind you, or even a lot of money. **It requires an intimate spiritual connection with God through Jesus Christ, knowing His Word, and walking in the power of His Spirit.**

According to Jesus in John 10:10, "The thief comes only to steal and kill and destroy; but I have come that you may have life, and have it more abundantly."

Christ revealed that Satan's primary purpose is expressed in the threefold area of **"stealing, killing and destroying."**

It has become extremely apparent that the three main tools that Satan uses that have unfortunately been proven successful are: **Delays, Distractions, and Disappointments.**

When things don't go your way or doors aren't opening as quick as you'd hoped for or you didn't get what you were seeking after, the forces of darkness really begin to turn your mind into a battlefield.

Satan's strategy then has been to bombard your mind with negative questions, accusations, frustrations, and then suggestive ideas **in the attempt to lead you astray, crush your spirit, conquer your faith, and destroy your life.**

Through his attacks and activities, he kills dreams and visions, crushes ideas and wounds spirits, destroys marriages, homes, relationships and careers, invades and subverts rightful thinking, steals peace and poisons minds, creates divisions and deceives hearts, entraps people into different addictions and bondages, directs people into debt and poverty, brings sickness and disease, seizes confidence and curses futures, masterminds hatred, and leads people straight to death and hell.

But Jesus declared that "I have come that you may have life, and have it more abundantly."

As a true believer, Christ has given you Eternal Life and placed The Life Of His Spirit inside of you.

As a child of God, you now have the untold or unlimited capacity of His grace, goodness, beauty, love, mercy, wisdom, joy, strength, authority, and power.

So in whatever way Satan and the forces of darkness attempt to operate in our midst, **as born-again, blood washed, Bible believing and Spirit led children of God,** we've been given absolute authority over them through Jesus Christ.

Jesus Christ conquered the devil, death, hell, and the grave through his death on the cross and his resurrection. He disarmed Satan and the forces of darkness and **obtained a name that is superior, mightier, and above all other names** whether in heaven, on the earth, or underneath the earth.

Through the name of Jesus Christ, you now have the ability and authority to resist the devil, to bind the forces of darkness, to rebuke him, to tear down his strongholds, to destroy his plans, and to frustrate his counsel and activities.

But again, the way you live your life and conduct spiritual warfare reveals if you believe **"The Most High God or the most low devil."**

So, who do you believe?

9

"When God Is All You Have, You've Just Learned That He's All You Really Need"

In 1st Samuel chapter 14, we are given an amazing account that demonstrates that one with God is an overwhelming majority when it comes to doing His will. So, often we today forget about The Power of God's Holy Spirit and what can be accomplished if we would just learn to depend on our Lord.

In 1st **Samuel 14: 6-7 NIV we read that** "Jonathan said to his young armor-bearer, "Come, let's go over to the outpost of those uncircumcised men. Perhaps the LORD will act in our behalf. Nothing can hinder the LORD from saving, whether by many or by few. "Do all that you have in mind," his armor-bearer said. "Go ahead; I am with you heart and soul."

Each time the roll call was taken, King Saul's army had diminished in size until all that remained were just a mere 600 men facing the Philistine army of multiple thousands. While the rest of Saul's soldiers either went into hiding from the enemy or fled the countryside, **faith rose up in the heart of Saul's son, Jonathan and he devised a plan of action.**

While his action was totally contrary to the normal laws of war because no military operation should be taken without the knowledge, approval and the command of its general, Jonathan didn't share his idea with his father Saul because he had lost touch with God. Nor did he make his idea public for he knew that others would discourage it because they were filled with fear and unbelief.

So, with his spirit having been stirred up by the Lord, he became fully persuaded and placed his confidence only in

God's divine presence and power instead of just mere human strength.

While Israel was greatly outnumbered by the enemy, Jonathan believed that the issue wasn't whether his army was many or few or if they were well organized or if they had great military weapons.

Jonathan believed that even though all he had was God, he believed that God was all that he needed. So he acted in faith, relying on God to save, deliver and help him achieve the victory against the enemy. And amazingly, his plan succeeded.

He, along with his sole faithful young armor bearer, climbed the steep cliffs on their hands and knees, then completely surprised the garrison of the enemy, which led to the entire confusion, panic and defeat of the Philistine army. Then those Israelite soldiers that were in hiding, seeing what was going on, received courage and came out of hiding to join in the battle and victory.

This entire story reveals that even if you're outnumbered, lacking the resources and the manpower to give you support, God will always direct the steps of those that acknowledge and put their complete trust in Him. There's so much biblical evidence which reveals or demonstrates that God will always move in a person's heart and lead them in unusual or unexpected ways, so **HE ALONE** will get the glory.

1st Corinthians 1:27 NIV says "But God chose the foolish things of the world to shame the wise; God chose the weak things of the world to shame the strong."

Things or individuals that others consider foolish, uneducated, lacking wealth or social skills, which are even ridiculed and rebuked by those who refer to themselves as being wiser, richer and more refined, **God will use to perform great exploits and bring others to shame.**

One humble person, whose heart is open and turned on to Christ, under the influence of The Holy Spirit of God, will be used to confound those who boast of their wisdom and accomplish things that others cannot attain or achieve.

<u>THEREFORE, HAVE FAITH IN GOD!</u>

Andrew Bills

10

"What's Holding You Back From Making Yourself Completely Available To God?"

Has God called you to do something but you make excuses and continue to procrastinate? Why are so many people afraid to step out in faith and do God's Will? Fear of the unknown, doubt, and unbelief are the major challenges in the minds of many believers. We as human beings always like to **"play it safe"** and want to know everything in advance and want God to move miraculously first before stepping out in faith.

I too had once struggled in this area as God had called me to full-time ministry. I had a very good job with lots of responsibility, but was working 6 and often 7 days a week doing 15 -16 hours each day. Doing God's will was always in my heart and mind, but I continued to procrastinate, making excuses, until one day I just couldn't take it any longer.

Then after crying aloud in the building and fully surrendering to The Lord, The Holy Spirit spoke strongly to my heart and said, **"Believe my Word and don't doubt in your heart!"** Then I left that job and I've never looked back since.

I encountered many naysayers along the way, but the blessings and grace of God were greater as I now continue to preach and teach the Word of God.

There are so many believers that have a burning passion to do something for the Lord or have a call to preach the Gospel globally, but they are afraid to step out in faith because of their job, their "benefits," and they are more worried about how their bills (car note, cell phone, rent/mortgage, insurance, light bill, water bill, etc.) are going to get paid rather than learning **how to**

fully yield themselves to Christ and trust Him to supply all their needs according to His riches in glory.

If you are passionate about winning souls for God's kingdom, **then stop worrying about how your bills will get paid and just start following Christ and pray for God's will and direction for your life.** Then pray about your finances, since it's usually the area that most people struggle with.

When you make Christ your priority and make yourself available for God to use, you will be surprised and amazed at what He will do in you, through you, by you, and with you.

In Luke 9: 57-62 we are given the story of 3 different individuals that Jesus dealt with regarding following Him.

Luke 9: 57-58 NIV says, "As they were walking along the road, a man said to him, 'I will follow you wherever you go.' Jesus replied, 'Foxes have dens and birds have nests, but the Son of Man has no place to lay his head.'"

This particular man was a Scribe, who was a teacher of the Law. It was clearly evident that Christ saw that his motivation was to acquire worldly gain and build his reputation, so Jesus tested his sincerity by informing him of the hardships that surrounded him, and it appears that he wasn't heard from again.

Then Luke 9:59-60 NIV says, "He said to another man, 'Follow me.' But he replied, 'Lord, first let me go and bury my father.' Jesus said to him, 'Let the dead bury their own dead, but you go and proclaim the kingdom of God.'"

Are you willing to follow The Lord even while going through the most trying circumstances? This man sought for a delay. **Procrastination!** Jesus wasn't against burying the dead. If this man really believed, he would've asked Christ to heal or raise his father from the dead. Jesus knew that if he returned back home, his friends might ridicule, oppose him, or present arguments that would prevent him from following Him.

Jesus taught that nothing should be allowed to divert the mind and be used as an excuse for not following him. Not even the death of a father and the sorrows of an afflicted family should be used to keep a person following Christ or to put off the purpose for becoming a Christian.

Our Lord was not speaking disrespectfully of or against burying the dead, but that it would be more advantageous for those who were spiritually dead to handle the last rites and that he should be more concerned about following Him. Since there were enough of his relatives there to take care of handling that burial, Jesus was revealing to him that there was no need why he should neglect the ministry of the gospel and attend to that affair.

Finally Luke 9: 61-62 NIV says, "Still another said, 'I will follow you, Lord; but first let me go back and say goodbye to my family.' Jesus replied, 'No one who puts a hand to the plow and looks back is fit for service in the kingdom of God.'"

Here is another who is willing to follow Christ, but he first must have a little time to talk with his friends about it and take time to set his household in order.

Again, when you make Christ your priority and make yourself available for God to use, you'll be surprised and amazed at what He will do in you, through you, by you, and with you in the mighty name of Jesus Christ, our Lord.

11

"Did You Know That Experience Is A Teacher, But You Don't Have To Let It Become Your Undertaker?"

We've all made bad decisions or wrongful choices, made mistakes, missed opportunities, or performed sinful activities. We've all experienced an unexpected tragedy, unforeseen sickness, or suffered some sort of misfortune in life. **We've all thought to ourselves or said out publicly at some point in life,** "If I had the sense back then, that I have today, things would've turned out differently."

Revelation 2:26 NIV says, "To him that overcomes and does my will to the end, I will give authority over the nations."

Jesus, in speaking to the church in Thyatria, initially began to commend this church, but then they allowed wicked seducers to enter and begin corrupting their fellowship. Christ began to call them to learn from their mistakes and to repent or He would rebuke, correct and punish them. If they would repent, then they would partake in the final triumph and be associated with Him in glory.

THANK GOD FOR HIS LOVE, MERCY, GRACE & FORGIVENESS THROUGH JESUS CHRIST! Now our lives should always be looking to Jesus Christ, walking in faith, listening to The Holy Spirit and daily learning how to overcome temptations, adversities, set-backs, oppositions, and hindrances as we stand on His Word.

All Christians should earnestly desire that their last works may be their best works as you are growing in His Grace. So let's continue to stand against the enemy that we may continue as overcomers and perform the will and works of Christ to the very end.

Jesus Christ is still able to save, deliver, strengthen, provide for, and help guide us through any darkness that you're experiencing.

12

"Are You Still Living In The Rear View Mirror?"

The rear view mirror in an automobile was designed for a driver to periodically take a quick glance at what's behind you or see what you've passed. **But it was never created for all of your attention to remain there.**

The front windshield is several times larger than the rear view mirror for an important purpose: To keep your attention on what's ahead and focus on where you're really trying to go.

Many won't go forward in their lives because they're pre-occupied with looking back instead of pressing forward. Others don't want to make changes because they're too comfortable with how things used to be.

Their past is familiar and they think more about what's behind them than about where they're heading and what will happen. If their eyes remain fixed to the rear view mirror of life, sooner or later they are bound to crash.

You are a liability to all who ride with you if you don't remain alert and see where you're going. Nobody wants to be involved with a driver whose always looking back or distracted with past events.

In Philippians 3:13-14 NASB, The Apostle Paul said, "Brethren, I do not regard myself as having laid hold of it yet; but one thing I do: forgetting what lies behind and reaching forward to what lies ahead, I press on toward the goal for the prize of the upward call of God in Christ Jesus."

Paul's metaphor is that of a runner in a Grecian race, running to win. In order to win, **the runner cannot afford to divert his**

mind nor attention away by stopping to look behind him to see how much ground he had passed over, the past difficulties he had to overcome, if a competitor had fallen, or to check out the locations of the other runners. He has to keep his eyes focused on the prize, control his breathing, extend every muscle and strain every nerve so that he might press onward to win his crown.

Each new day is God's gift to you and what you do with it is your offering back to Him, as well as a gift to yourself and your family. Each day He grants us His Grace and another chance to seize opportunities to make that day count towards eternity.

While there's nothing wrong with having cherished past memories, you must not allow the past to interfere with your pressing onward to win the prize. **Don't allow past sins to weigh you down or count you out.** Confess, repent and walk forward in the forgiveness of God and know the shed blood of Jesus Christ now covers your sins and they are remembered no more by God.

Don't look back upon worldly things or activities and start yearning after them like the Israelites did after the fleshpots in Egypt. Stop looking back with regrets. Looking back can lead to you drawing back, turning around, going off in the wrong direction and crashing.

Some of the things you once valued, pursued or trusted in before your conversion and new relationship in Christ need now to be dropped, renounced, discarded and counted as dung, as you're now running in the new race that's set before you. Have faith in God and press on to your prize, and with His help, know that you will make it.

13

"Why Do Some Find It Easier To Listen To Others Than To Take God At His Word?"

Johnny was rushed to the hospital, diagnosed by the attending physician, and given the following definite medication instructions: *"Take this medicine without fail three times a day until it's all gone."* So without giving it a second thought, he completely followed his doctor's orders until he totally recovered.

Well, just as it took time for Johnny's medicine to take effect, **you need to give God's Word in your life time to take effect and render changes in your circumstances.** If you'll give His Word the same opportunity that Johnny gave his doctor's prescription, then your life will never be the same again.

Why is it that people find it easier to listen and believe their doctors, lawyers, and even their friend's advice instead of taking God at His Word? Well, some have suggested that waiting on the Lord isn't easy. Secondly, many have placed their confidence in something or someone that they can physically see rather than trusting in an invisible or distant god.

While waiting on the Lord isn't easy or at times may even appear to be very uncomfortable, the scriptures are empathically clear that God always hears and answers prayer and **what you truly need is a daily dosage of The Word of God into your heart and spirit.**

Secondly, if you believe that He's too distant from you, it's only because you've moved or turned away from Him. **He will be as close to you as you will allow Him to be in your life.**

Too often people want a quick fix, an immediate remedy cure, or even a magic wand to be waved over them with the special magician's words, **"abracadabra,"** without having to change your life and repent from your sins.

But having faith, feeding on and learning to take God at His Word is just what's been divinely prescribed by our **Heavenly Father, who is THE GREAT PHYSICIAN.**

Now, at times our attention can be misdirected, selfish, lustful, or so fixed upon our desire or need so much that our focus actually shifts away from seeking Christ to seeking things. **God IS NOT** in the business of just handing out gifts, **HE'S IN** the business of saving, delivering, and changing lives. **And The Word of God will keep you from sin, or sin will keep you from the Word of God.**

Remember the words that The Holy Spirit declared in Hebrews 11:6 NIV, "Those that come to God must first believe that He is and that He's a rewarder of those that diligently seek him."

Some situations may exist where God waits only because the timing isn't right or when He wants to stretch and mature our faith. While He's orchestrating in your life and affairs, certain things may need to be rightly positioned or altered. **While in some other instances, other people's thinking may even need to be changed towards you.** At other times, many have wrongful, selfish, or impure motives or are persisting in a lifestyle of disobedience or living in habitual sin and God is calling for repentance and turning to Him.

While these are just a few reasons for delays, one thing is absolutely certain, that faith in God's Word and trust in The Lord Jesus Christ are needed. **So continue to stand in faith and learn to always take God at His Word.**

14

"Are You Afraid To Believe God Because Of The Opinions Of Others?"

When you are afraid to believe God because of the opinion of others, you literally have become a prisoner of those that you want to please. But, it's more important for you to learn to please God than to be careful of what you say to people and who you're saying it to when you initially decide to step out in faith.

Sharing your personal goals, ministry vision or business dreams to the wrong people can have a crippling or devastating affect before it even gets off the ground and has a chance to blossom.

Just because someone makes inquiries, doesn't mean that they are concerned or care about you and want you to succeed. Our world is full of lost dreams and unrealized visions because of the criticism from others, even from some that you've attempted to please.

In John chapter 9, we read the amazing story of Jesus healing a man that was born blind on the Sabbath day that reveals this truth. After spitting on the ground and making clay from the dirt, Jesus rubbed the mud on the eyes of the blind man and instructed him to go wash in a certain pool. As a result of his obedience, the man miraculously received his sight. But because of this taking place on the Sabbath day, along with their hatred for Jesus, many began to deny that a miracle had even taken place and referred to Christ as a sinner.

So in John 9: 25-27 NIV, we read that after numerous inquiries, interviews, interrogations and accusations from neighbors, family members and the overzealous religious Pharisees, the former blind man completely exhausted and anguished because of their lack of joy over the fact that he had been marvelously healed, replied, "Whether he is a sinner or not, I don't know. One thing I do know. I was blind but now I see!" Then they asked him again, "What did he do to you? How did he open your eyes?" He answered, "I have told you already and you did not listen. Why do you want to hear it again? Do you want to become his disciples too?"

After hearing of his miraculous encounter with Jesus, they continued to show disregard in their attempts to intimidate, ensnare, discredit his testimony and confuse him. Overwhelmed by their unbelief and their willingness to reject his experience, he stung them with some strong sarcastic questions.

Today, many just don't want to hear the facts, while others are just jealous of anything that you'll try to rise up to try and accomplish. Therefore, you shouldn't reveal, share or release anything until The Holy Spirit of God instructs you too. Their words of discouragement will be used by Satan as a tool to distract you from what God has placed in your heart to do and make you start questioning your instructions from God.

So, it doesn't matter what your parents, relatives, neighbors or even your best friends will say to you. **At the end of the day, God is going to hold you accountable for what you did with His Son, Jesus Christ.**

Obstacles will come but God will only allow them to reveal if you're more concerned about the opinion of others or about trusting Christ and doing His Will. Will you dare to be different and stand on God's Word? Are you going to listen to the opinions of man or will you place your confidence in God?

Finally, after being cast out of the synagogue and being ostracized by everyone, **Jesus found him,** and the man worshipped Christ because of His awesome love and grace. And God gave him a new beginning.

THEREFORE, HAVE FAITH IN GOD!

15

"How Can We Be Sure That God Will Keep His Promises?"

In The New Testament, **all of God's promises are predicated on what Jesus Christ did on Calvary and God's faithfulness to keep His Word.** So, whether you realize it or not, God has a very lengthy and faithful history of stepping into dark, negative and impossible situations and changing things.

Now first, The Lord's character IS OUR guarantee. Since HE IS HOLY, He's always perfect, never changing, always truthful and all-powerful so HE CANNOT LIE OR NEVER FAIL to keep His Word.

Secondly, His sacrifice on the cross and His Resurrection from the dead IS DEFINITE & ETERNAL PROOF of His Love and that HE ALWAYS Keeps His Word.

In Mark 13:31 Jesus Himself declared, "Heaven and earth will pass away, but my words will not pass away." This statement is one of the strongest expressions ever spoken in human language revealing His divine authority and superiority over any and all forces, situations and conditions.

Now, although The Lord's unchangeable promises are wonderful expressions of His love, mercy and grace towards us in this rapidly changing world, it must be clearly stated that we also have certain responsibilities along the way.

In John 15:7 Jesus said, "If you abide in me, and my words abide in you, ask whatever you wish, and it will be done for you."

This means that when His Words are ablaze in our hearts and we walk by faith in them, that they just won't be merely remembered but will govern our conduct, affections and lifestyle. Then you shall see your prayers being answered to bring glory to our Heavenly Father. **So ask in faith, walk in obedience, stand on His promise and wait on The Lord.**

For all of the promises of God made through Christ, relate to the forgiveness of sin to the seeker, the sanctification of his people, His support in times of temptation and trial, His deliverance, healing, strength and guidance in distressful situations, His peace in death, and eternal glory beyond the grave. **All of these are made through our Redeemer and none of these shall ever fail.**

<u>THEREFORE, HAVE FAITH IN GOD!</u>

16

"PRAYER –
That Makes Things Change!"

In July of 1994, Cindy, a pastor's wife in Arkansas, was confronted in her home by a pistol-wielding burglar. The unknown man who surprised her when she came in to answer the phone ripped the cord from the wall and ordered her into a closet. She was obviously fearful for her life, but didn't panic. To the shock of the gunman, Cindy immediately fell to her knees and began to pray for God's Help. **Even more stunned was he when she boldly asked if she could pray for him!** She proceeded to tell him about Christ's love and expressed her forgiveness for his actions.

Apparently this was more than the robber bargained for, and began to break into tears as he knelt and prayed with her. To her relief, the man then yelled out the window to a woman waiting in a pickup: "We've got to unload all of this stuff. This is a Christian home and we can't do this to them."

Cindy remained on her knees in prayer, while her furniture was being returned. The man then used a shirt to wipe off his fingerprints, apologized and departed, even leaving his gun behind!

This true story vividly illustrates how willing God is to intervene in behalf of His children when asked, as it says in **James 5:17,** "The effectual fervent prayer of a righteous man avails much."

This refers to prayer as being intense, energetic, earnest, heartfelt, sincere, and persevering instead of being cold, routine, lifeless and wavering as if there were no vitality, faith or enthusiasm in it. **Consistent, earnest and continual prayer**

will always prevail with a revelation of God's love, grace, power, and victory in your life. This is the kind of prayer that reveals a real relationship with The Lord.

It's totally beyond explanation that God, the great **I AM** and our loving Heavenly Father, has made Himself available and placed Himself at the disposal to all those that earnestly turn to Him and call on His name. While we are told that prayer works, we never will fully understand the fullness of God's Grace behind prayer.

There's a difference between praying to God and **experiencing God through prayer.** Again, prayer is not just something you routinely or haphazardly do. **It's the place where you decide to meet God.**

Prayer is one of your **"totally unequalled"** weapons by which you can pierce through any darkness and overcome any obstacle as you come before His throne, calling upon The Lord Jesus Christ, knowing that He loves you.

THEREFORE, HAVE FAITH IN GOD!

17

"How Great Is Your Desire To See God Move In Your Life?"

The miraculous works of God are always the result of a deep, inner and insatiable desire for a change. God isn't moved or compelled to orchestrate in our hearts or affairs because a person quickly mumbles some **"off the cuff"** prayer without any thought behind it.

No, God is always moved to intervene for those who diligently, passionately, intimately and faithfully seek Him. **And this kind of prayer usually involves both sacrificial time and hard work, as one seeks to pierce through their darkness, prevail through their pains, and persevere right into the throne room of God's grace.**

We are given an excellent example of this in **1st Samuel 1: 9-18** in the brief story of Hannah. Hannah was childless and grieved; she couldn't tolerate being barren any longer, so she pleaded and poured out her soul before God.

Here In verse 11, Hannah's prayers were cried out as they were mingled with her tears, "LORD Almighty, if you will only look on your servant's misery and remember me, and not forget your servant, but give her a son. Then I will give him to the LORD for all the days of his life, and no razor will ever be used on his head."

Her vow here implies that he would be consecrated to the Lord from his infancy to his death, to serve him, and minister unto him in the sanctuary, fully dedicating him to the tabernacle service; and that he should not only act as a Levite, but as a Nazarite, on whose head no razor should ever pass.

Being unwilling to let the Lord go until she received some sort of promise or satisfaction, she continued praying in her heart. In the temple as she prayed, her distorted appearance and uplifted eyes and hands were observed by the priest, who not hearing any words but seeing her lips move, initially though she was intoxicated from wine.

Then in verses 15-16 Hannah answers, "Not so, my lord," Hannah replied, "I am a woman who is deeply troubled. I have not been drinking wine or beer; I was pouring out my soul to the LORD. Do not take your servant for a wicked woman; I have been praying here out of my great anguish and grief."

Out of the abundance of her heart, Hannah began to vent and make known her desires to The Lord. And the Lord remembered Hannah and gave her the power to conceive and she brought forth a son and called his name Samuel.

Let us be reminded of the promise given in Matthew 6:6 by Jesus himself, "But when you pray, go into your room, close the door and pray to your Father, who is unseen. Then your Father, who sees what is done in secret, will reward you."

Is there some place where you can go and have your secret devotions? Is there a place where you may be alone with God to pour out your heart? If you really want answers and need God to hear your petitions, you will create the place and the time needed to really get before the Lord, like Hannah, to pour out your heart and listen for his response in your spirit. You will give the Lord your time and make him a priority. **There's a reward, power and anointing that comes out of prevailing and persistent prayer that cannot be derived from anywhere else.**

Remember the words from James 4:3 which declare that "You have not because you ask not or ask amiss." When you ask, don't ask with the wrong motives of self-indulgence or carnal gratification, that you may spend what you get on your pleasures. On some occasions even if you do pray, you do it only that you may live in splendor to pamper your lusts. **No,**

always come before His presence with the right intentions and purpose of heart.

Remember, whatever's ahead of you is never as great as the power that's with you. And according to His gracious promises, He will move in your life and affairs, **through the mighty name of Jesus Christ.**

<u>**THEREFORE, HAVE FAITH IN GOD!**</u>

18

"Are You Trusting The Lord Or Taking Matters Into Your Own Hands?"

Do you really believe that God can handle your situation? **Then why do so many people try to develop and activate a "<u>back up plan</u>?"** Why are you always trying to figure things out instead of listening to Him guide and direct you? Why do some try to manipulate, intervene, substitute or help out after declaring that they've taken all of their burdens to The Lord? **Are they not leaving them there for God to resolve?**

On the night of His arrest, Jesus told his disciples that he would be betrayed, arrested and killed. But He also told them about His Resurrection, the coming of The Holy Spirit, the new intimacy they would have with God and His Second Coming.

Jesus had just spent a brief time in agonizing prayer, when soldiers led by Judas came to arrest Him in the Garden of Gethsemane. Just as they advanced to seize and apprehend Christ, **Peter purposely thought that he had to somehow defend his Lord to prevent His arrest.**

In John 18:10 -11 NIV says, "Then Simon Peter, who had a sword, drew it and struck the high priest's servant, cutting off his right ear. (The servant's name was Malchus.). Jesus commanded Peter, "Put your sword away! Shall I not drink the cup the Father has given me?"

Why did Peter draw his sword in the first place? **After hearing The Lord's words, why was he trying to activate "<u>plan B</u>?"** Didn't Peter realize that by trying to defend or trying to rescue Jesus was to prevent the perfect will of God from occurring and keep salvation from being made available to the world? **Had he** not heard all of the promises and benefits that Jesus stated would happen through His death and resurrection?

The injured servant's name was Malchus. His name is not mentioned by any of the other gospel writers, nor did they reveal who was the disciple that delivered the blow by swinging the sword. Only John provided us with the full account. Now regardless, whether Peter was just not good at handling the sword or whether God turned Peter's aim aside and only permitted the ear to be taken off in order to present this opportunity of giving them more proof of his Divinity in working an astonishing miracle on the occasion, we just don't know.

But Jesus rebuked Peter's rash, foolish, selfish, dangerous and unnecessary action and told him **that if He wanted He could have summoned His Father to send more than 12 legions of angels to protect and deliver Him.** Peter's bold imprudent action also had placed all the lives of the remaining disciples at risk, had not Christ immediately intervened by touching and healing the servant's severed ear.

Yes, even though they came to destroy His life, Jesus Christ came to save the lives of all sinners that would call upon Him. And then make the continual difference by orchestrating in the affairs and lives of all believers.

So, can you name a time that **The Lord IS NOT** completely worthy of your confidence or trust? You are exhorted and encouraged to trust in or rely on Him **AT ALL TIMES** and not try to handle matters on you own. **Are you standing on God's Infallible Word or are you busy trying to create your own back plan known as "plan B?"**

In times of adversity, he can cause you to prosper. In times of affliction, He's promised never to leave you or forsake you. In times of temptation, you'll find that His Grace is sufficient for you. **In times of darkness, He will be your Light and guide you through your wilderness season.** In times of danger, He's able to protect us. In times of need, He's promised to supply us and make ways out of no ways. In times of doubt or uncertainty, He's able to birth hope in your heart and give you peace of mind and bring you through the most difficult situations. **<u>SO, HAVE FAITH IN GOD!</u>**

Andrew Bills

19

"What Should You Do When "Goliath" Comes?"

I have a sign mounted on the wall in front of my desk that says, **"Don't tell God how big your mountain is; tell the mountain how big your God is!"** The sign is there to remind me that we all will face some giants, but what we need to do is respond in faith when we're confronted by them.

You may want to run away in fear, you may try to avoid them and act as if they'll just go away. **But the giants won't just go away; they must be confronted and dealt with. And they can be overcome and defeated!** As you journey through life, battles are inevitable, so you must learn to depend on Christ, take God at His Word and believe Him for your breakthrough and victory.

In 1st Samuel chapter 17, we read a story many of us remember from our youth. While we've all heard of young brave David and confrontational evil Goliath, **The Holy Spirit of God has a few things to reveal, remind and encourage you.**

"Goliath" represents any damnable hard time, any adverse or abusive circumstance, any negative persecution or stressful situation, any overwhelming financial crisis, any physical, mental, emotional or spiritual painful condition, any unshakable destructive bad habit or sin, or any surrounding demonic activity or satanic entrapment. **Your "Goliath" will confront you, challenge you, oppose you, discourage you and will attempt to defeat you!**

You must know that, no matter what "Goliath" confronts you, the love from the cross and the grace from Christ's empty tomb are MORE than enough to encourage, sustain and persuade you! In trusting Christ and taking God at His

Word you will daily realize that The Holy Spirit in you will enable you to become a **"giant killer"** and that it's time to TRUST GOD.

In 1st Samuel 17:26, David strongly asks, "Who *is* this uncircumcised Philistine, that he should defy the armies of the living God?"

After considering God's glorious promises and his recent experiences of divine assistance in killing the bear and the lion, David was determined that he would go into battle **with the things that had always worked for him in the past.** David knew that God, who had always come through in the past, was the very same God who would still come through in this new present situation.

Can you believe that the very same Lord that brought you through trials and challenges before will do it again? The very same Lord that saved you is more than able to yet keep you, as you look to Him and stand on His Word.

Initially, David was criticized and even opposed by those he thought supported him. But he trusted God. Often, **we too must learn that if God is all we have, He's really all we need.** So, we must rise and go forward in faith in Jesus Christ and know we can trust Him.

David walked into that valley into an impossible situation only because he knew God had been faithful and would remain faithful. God specializes in working in dark, dire, and impossible situations, and David believed God would not fail him in that new crisis and he won't fail you either. <u>**For if God be for you, who or what can be against you?**</u>

You may not see your giants physically fall the very instant you exercise faith in God. <u>**But, don't let that cause you to lose hope!**</u> For you often cannot believe what the eyes of your flesh see. But, **you can always believe what the eyes of faith see because we walk by faith and not by sight.**

So, even if it may look like you're outgunned, outnumbered and in an impossible situation, just remember that it looked that way for Shadrach, Meshach and Abednego. It looked that way for Daniel. It looked that way for the disciples when the storm raged outside their ship. **It certainly looked that way for Jesus as he was lifted high upon that cross.** But, God had the final **"say-so"** in each of these life changing experiences.

If you want to see the giants in your life lying dead at your feet, you must do as David did. He believed God was greater than any giant that he could ever face. **He believed that the same Lord that brought him through challenges in the past still reigned on high,** and the same sources (prayer, faith, praise, The Word of God and The Holy Spirit) that he used under prior conditions, were always available and would work under any new challenge! **And that's still true for you today as you confront the Goliaths in your own life.**

<u>**THEREFORE, HAVE FAITH IN GOD!**</u>

20

"How Secret Are Your Secret Sins?"

The Bible talks about the wisdom of this world being foolishness to God. This is clearly seen in the life of anyone who thinks or even pretends to believe that they can 'put one over' on God. **You will only come to realize that secret sins on earth are open scandals in Heaven.**

Years ago, there was a man in my church that was having multiple sexual affairs. He actually believed that neither his wife, family, friends or anyone else in the church would ever find out. **Imagine the grief, humiliation, embarrassment, and shame as it all was discovered.** He additionally learned that his **so-called "secret sins"** brought a world of hurt to others that were involved in his life.

There are those that actually think, believe or act as if The Lord can't see their sin if they try and hide it under a cloak of darkness or perform it in a locked room. **But can any of your activities be concealed from his all-seeing eye? Can anyone entertain displeasing thoughts and believe that God won't know the intentions of your heart?**

Jeremiah 23:24 NIV says, "Can anyone hide in secret places so that I cannot see him?" declares the LORD. "Do not I fill heaven and earth?" declares the LORD."

Then in Hebrews 4:13 NIV The Holy Spirit says, "Nothing in all creation is hidden from God's sight. Everything is uncovered and lay bare before the eyes of him to whom we must give account."

If you try to hide yourself or attempt to cover up or keep secret your activities, **the devil will additionally expose you to**

further ruin your character, credibility, respectability and relationships.

No attempt to disguise yourself will profit you. And there's no art of concealment that you can entertain or conduct that will hide you from God or prevent you from reaping what you've sown.

In conclusion, just remember these final words from God through the Prophet Isaiah in **Isaiah 29:15 NIV which declare,** "Woe to those who go to great depths to hide their plans from the LORD, who do their work in darkness and think, **"Who sees us? Who will know?"**

<u>Therefore, Have Faith In God And Walk Upright Before Him And You'll Have Greater Rewards.</u>

21

"What Should You Do If God Seems Silent Or Absent?"

Does it seem as if God has packed up, moved far away, and left no forwarding address for you? Are you going through a painful situation and you are not sensing His presence, promptings or hearing His voice? **Have you been praying to The Lord and all that you're getting back is "silence?"**

I recently read in a newsletter the following words, "When you are going through something hard and wonder where God is remember, the teacher is always quiet during the test."

While that's a cute and humorous saying, the truth of the matter is that many people believe that **"silence is painful when it comes to God in our lives."** For it often leaves a person confused, agonizing with uncertainties entering into their minds and even wondering if God has completely abandoned them.

In 1st Kings Chapter 19, we read the story of the mighty Prophet Elijah. He had just been used by God to perform a great miracle which resulted with the destruction of 450 false prophets of Baal on Mt. Carmel. But afterwards, when he received word that the wicked Queen Jezebel wanted to destroy his life, he fled away, complained about how he was being treated and began to think that God had now abandoned him by being silent.

Then in 1st Kings 19:10 NIV, Elijah cries out in sheer anguish, "I have been very zealous for the LORD God Almighty. The Israelites have rejected your covenant, torn down your altars, and put your prophets to death with the sword. I am the only one left, and now they are trying to kill me too."

We see in this passage of Scripture that Elijah's concerns were not true. Elijah thought God was silent and that he was the only one left standing for The Lord. **God who is never silent** revealed to Elijah that He had an army waiting in the wings, ensuring Elijah that he was not alone. **In 1st Kings 19:18 God informed him** "Yet I have left me seven thousand in Israel, all the knees which have not bowed unto Baal, and every mouth which hath not kissed him."

God is **NOT** indifferent to the needs or the dangers that face His Children. **He is always mindful of the tears and cries of His people.**

If you're not sensing or hearing God's voice in your life, then the very first thing you must do is to examine your heart and make sure that the following sins are **NOT** in your life:

That you are **not** harboring secret sins, that you are **not** filled with anger, that you are **not** full of unbelief, that you are **not** carrying grudges and are **not** walking in unforgiveness, that you are **not** living a rebellious lifestyle or **not** following a rebellious spirit, that you **don't have** the wrong image or portrait of God, that you're **not** too busy to spend intimate quality time in God's Word.

But, if you **ARE** living a prayer-less life instead of a prayerful life and if your love for the world is still greater than your love for God, then know that it's time to repent and make changes in your heart.

Whenever it may appear that God is silent, **HE NEVER IS.** What may look like silence or inactivity is just **Our Lord working things out both inside of us and orchestrating in our affairs.** He's then allowing you the opportunity and privilege to draw closer to Him and listen to **"the still small voice"** of The Holy Spirit and receive a fresh revelation of His Love, Grace and Power as you **STAND ON HIS WORD.**

As you're standing, don't panic and be moved by what you see. Standing is your statement of faith, even if you're still under pressure, that you believe God's Word. Standing means that you've set yourself to hold fast to the Word and Promises of God with the confidence that He will do what He said He would in His Word.

Yes, there's always going to be times where we as believers will have to **STAND IN FAITH, WALK IN OBEDIENCE AND ENDURE HARDSHIPS** as we wait on The Lord. But rest in the assurance of His gracious promise, **as declared in Hebrews 13:5, where He promised** "I'll never leave you nor forsake you."

Andrew Bills

22

"Do You Have A Plan To Win Or Are You Just Trying To Survive The Day?"

Walking by faith doesn't mean not having a plan or goal in sight and aimlessly just tip-toeing through life. **According to Hebrews 11:1,** "Faith is the substance of things hoped for, the evidence of things not seen." **This reveals that God wants you to plan and stand, so you can thrive and not just survive.**

Good goals and plans require vision, dedication, planning, energy, discipline, perseverance and of course, God's Grace. **All these elements go along with a day-by-day strategy of trusting Christ and standing on His Word, as you're walking and working in faith to get things done.**

Often, your mission may include the involvement or participation of others to see your dreams come to life. But, first remember that you are **NOT** prepared to win if you don't have a plan of action, a goal in view or a purpose in mind.

When we started our outreach ministry activities, it was without any financial back-up or support partners or staffing. As we stepped out in faith, with our vision plan written down in front of our eyes, we've seen The Lord do great and mighty things and saw new doors start to open.

God wants you to lift up your eyes and aim high and allow His Holy Spirit to help enable you to perform your task at hand. Don't allow any adversities to blow your ship off the course that has been charted. **In order to avoid the dangerous riptides and sharp rocks, you must know where you want to go and how to safely get there.**

If you're going to drive across the country, shouldn't you have a destination in mind and a reliable map or GPS? If you're going to build yourself a new home, isn't it wisdom to have a blueprint first drawn up? Those without a set goal or plan in mind simply just wake up every morning with hope to make it through the day. And at its conclusion, they're left feeling overwhelmed and discouraged because of their lack of direction and empty achievements. **"Don't You Deserve More?"**

23

"If Something Is Done In The Name Of Jesus, Does That Always Mean That Jesus Approves?"

<u>No, it does not</u>! Our world is filled with people who just want to be seen, along with fakers, imposters, false prophets, con-artists, wolves in sheep clothing and deceivers, who's only motives have been to **"<u>fleece the flock</u>,"** to promote their own selfish agendas and to deceive the people. There have been many terrible things occur throughout the history of the church that are clear deviations from the teachings of Christ and His Apostles, performed by **"<u>spiritual gold-diggers</u>"** that have used the name of Jesus Christ in unimaginable ways.

They have wrecked homes, destroyed families, seized assets, stole from widows, broken relationships, split churches, and caused multitudes of others to blaspheme God, through their selfish interests, false prophesying, deceptive tricks, phony healings, and fake anointed miracles, all while invoking the name of The Lord. That's the reason that you must learn and study the Word of God, be lead of The Holy Spirit and have an intimate fellowship with Christ yourself, **that you might be able to discern or distinguish frauds and not fall prey to their deceptive antics.**

In Matthew 7: 22-23 Jesus said, "Many will say to me on that day, 'Lord, Lord, did we not prophesy in your name and in your name drive out demons and in your name perform many miracles?' Then I will tell them plainly, 'I never knew you. Away from me, you evildoers!'"

What an awful picture it is, that people who claimed to cast out devils, on judgment day, will themselves be cast to the devil, in the Lake of Fire for all eternity.

In Acts 10: 13-16 NIV God allowed the following story to become publicly witnessed and recorded in scripture to be a warning to many…. It says, "Some Jews who went around driving out evil spirits tried to invoke the name of the Lord Jesus over those who were demon-possessed. They would say, "In the name of the Jesus whom Paul preaches, I command you to come out." Seven sons of Sceva, a Jewish chief priest, were doing this. One day the evil spirit answered them, "Jesus I know, and Paul I know about, but who are you?" Then the man who had the evil spirit jumped on them and overpowered them all. He gave them such a beating that they ran out of the house naked and bleeding."

These Jews, who wandered from place to place, thought they could conduct exorcisms by merely duplicating Paul's words or actions. So they thought, if they could use the name of Jesus, just like the magic expression **"ab-ra-ca-da-bra,"** then they would have the same effect as The Apostle Paul. For they then believed it would become a wealthy source of income for them because of all the demonic individuals throughout that land.

Satan knows if Christ in dwelling in your life, if you're being led of The Holy Spirit, walking in the anointing and if you have credibility with God. The powers of darkness know if you have a personal relationship with Christ and have **"Son-ship Rights of Authority."**

These seven brothers found out the hard way that one demon possessed man with extraordinary power and rage, could overpower, strip them of their clothing, beat them shamefully and have them running down the street naked, wounded and bleeding. These impostors could not work miracles, and after they exposed themselves to the rage of evil spirits, their failure only served to extend the power of the gospel. Fear fell on all of the people, so that others were deterred from making such further attempts.

Regardless if some deceivers or imposters are having large assemblies of people, are financially prosperous in raising offerings or selling their products and seem as if they are getting away, **THEY WILL NOT CONTINUE TO STAND.**

The Lord Jesus Christ will have the final **"say-so"** or final word in every individual's life. And it should be your greatest desire to hear our Lord Jesus Christ say **"WELL DONE MY GOOD AND FAITHFUL SERVANT."**

Andrew Bills

24

"How Can I Overcome My Fears Through Faith In Jesus Christ?"

2nd Timothy 1:7 says, "For God hath not given us the spirit of fear; but of power, and of love, and of a sound mind."

Are you praying and believing God in faith and it doesn't appear as if anything spiritual, encouraging, positive or supernatural is happening? Are you experiencing on-going pressures? Here's a little illustration that will assist you in seeing Satan as **"the defeated foe that he is."**

When I was 7 years old, my dad built a chicken coop in the back yard and on one particular occasion, he told me to come outside to watch and learn. So I followed him out into the yard and into the chicken coop.

Once outside, he told me to catch one of the chickens. In the chicken yard there were several hens, but many more baby chicks. I ran around trying to catch one of these chickens and boy, could they move fast! After many attempts and much laughter from my dad, I finally caught one and brought it to him.

Then I asked him, **"What do you want me to do with this chick?"** He said, **"We're going to ring its neck and have it for dinner."** I laughed because I thought he was joking, but before I knew it, he brutally snapped off the neck of that chicken. Then, in total shock, I watched as its headless body flopped and moved around all over the place, for what I thought were hours, but in truth was only a few moments. Then it completely stopped moving and lay still.

Immediately, I flew into the house and watched from the window terrified. My father yelled to me, **"It's all right, the** chick is dead; it can't hurt you!" And he continued to laugh. But in my mind **(and my mind was the only one that seemed to matter)** that chick acted as if it was not only still alive, but mad and even coming after me! So, I ran and hid. My dad proceeded to pick it up, then walked away to prepare it for dinner.

Needless to say, even at dinner, I continued to stare at the chicken. Even though it was fully cooked, seasoned with gravy, and laying in dressing, I still thought it would move and come after me.

<u>**It took time for my mind to become released or freed from its control.**</u> And throughout my years and experiences in ministry, I've discovered that many people today are just like I was in this brief childhood illustration.

They're having difficulties fully realizing that Christ defeated Satan on Calvary and that the Resurrection is the full proof of Christ's Victory and Satan's Defeat. **It was there that Christ snapped the neck of Satan and he was defeated once and for all. Since then Satan has been put under the feet of all believers through the death, resurrection and ascension of Jesus Christ.**

Satan is now like the headless body of that chick that I was afraid of as a young child. Down through the centuries, people have been controlled by fear, by the movements or the flopping of a headless and defeated foe. **You need to know that the devil only has the power over you that you, as a believer give him through fear and allow Him to have.**

Remember, I ran because I thought he was going to get me... <u>**FEAR**</u>! Or even worse, while sitting at the dinner table, it was still through the controlling element of <u>**FEAR**</u> that I was continuing to be firmly held captive, blinded and paralyzed in my mind. This is our major battleground and we must renew our mind daily in the word of God, which acts as a sword against the wiles of the devil.

Satan will always try to enlarge, magnify and worsen the situation that you're facing. But, we need to see the devil as **"The defeated foe that he is."** Trust in the Lord and take the limits off of God. Stand firmly on His Promises and Christ will see you through.

THEREFORE, HAVE FAITH IN GOD!

25

"Do You Want To Develop A Victorious Attitude?"

The brief story was told of a husband and wife entering into a small plane which they piloted. After strapping themselves into their seats and immediately after the take-off, the wife heard the sound of a rattle and found a live and deadly rattlesnake in the cockpit with them, directly by her feet.

In a great panic, she told her husband and he shouted, **"Don't worry honey, snakes can't handle high altitudes, so I'll take the plane up a little bit higher."**

So after immediately climbing up a few thousand feet he said, **"Honey what's happening now?"** She nervously replied, **"The snake is starting to curl up into a ball or small circle."**

So he shouted a second time, **"I'll take the plane up a little bit higher"** and he pulled back on the throttle and climbed upward a few more thousand feet.

Once again he said, **"Honey, what's happening now?"**

And she replied, **"it's curled up into a tighter ball, its tongue is hanging out of its mouth, it's having trouble breathing, its eyes have rolled upwards into its head and its body is starting to shake."**

Again he shouted, **"Hold on and I'll take the plane up a little bit higher."** So, after climbing upwards another few thousand feet to an even higher elevation, he again asked, **"Honey, what's happening now?"**

She excitedly responded, **"Nothing! That snake is now DEAD! It's no longer a danger or a threat to us."** And she opened a little side window and threw its lifeless body out of the plane.

Are you aware that Satan cannot stand or survive the high altitude of your praise? Or that an increased elevation of prayer, study of God's Word and obedience to Christ will heighten or lift your attitude and destroy the works of the enemy in your life? **One of the most important steps in learning how to develop a victorious attitude is discovering the importance of Praising The Lord.**

Through praise, you'll sense a new burst of spiritual energy and receive new insight as your time with God both increases and becomes more intimate. You'll begin to sense the presence of The Lord, feel the pulse of His heartbeat and hear His voice speaking to your heart. It will appear as if you're walking around on higher ground.

Acts 16: 25-26 says, "At midnight Paul and Silas prayed and sang praises unto God and the prisoner heard them. And suddenly there was a great earthquake, so that the foundations of the prison were shaken and immediately all the doors were opened and everyone's bands were loosed."

It has been said, "<u>**That when praises go up, blessings come down.**</u>" Praise to our Lord always results in piercing through the surrounding darkness and see the invisible hand of God mightily moving in your midst. So whatever you do, don't give up, **<u>JUST CLIMB HIGHER</u>**. True worship is your way of attacking back.

Remember, the next time that fear, temptation, or any type of adversity comes knocking at your door, **LET FAITH ANSWER IT AND BREAKTHRU IN PRAISE TO THE LORD JESUS CHRIST.**

26

"Hurdles –
How Should They Be Viewed?"

Hurdles, we all shall face them. But regardless whether they'll appear as small bumps in the road or large gaping challenges, **BELIEVERS MUST LEARN TO VIEW THEM only as barriers that must be crossed.** Then once leaped over, we should forever remember them as an added testimony or a trophy in our life's experience.

In retrospect, some of the faced hurdles that I originally thought would definitely kill me only increased my faith and stretched my endurance as I trusted God.

In Isaiah 40:31 NIV God says "but those who trust in the LORD will renew their strength. They will soar on wings like eagles; they will run and not grow weary, they will walk and not be faint."

Though The Holy Spirit of God may remain invisible or appear to be silent, **He renews, re-invigorates, strengthens and sustains us at times when we feel we're too tired to run, walk, crawl or even carry on.** This verse reveals that God created us to be resilient, but only if we rely on Him as we run forward.

Just as a good long distance runner must steady his pace as he moves his body with speed, he must control his breathing by remaining calm and focused as he continues on his journey. **And just like this athlete,** you must keep your head lifted up, back straight, get rid of fear, not worry about the road ahead, feel the wind beneath your wings and soar beyond your expectations.

This passage reveals that you are to wait for his help and expect your deliverance through Christ. **Now, waiting doesn't imply**

inactivity or lack of personal exertion. No it only implies to trust in our salvation, through Him. **The Hebrew word means to change, to alter, to revive, to renew, to cause to flourish again, to increase, and to be restored.** It means that the people of God who trust in him shall become strong in faith, able to contend with their spiritual foes, to gain the victory over their sins, and to perform their Christian duties despite the trials in life, all without complaining, fainting or surrendering.

Like fresh feathers on a molting eagle, you shall be renewed as if experiencing youthfulness again, and you will rise and ascend to new heights or elevations, throughout your communion with God.

Remember, if you go forward in your own strength you shall faint and utterly fall. But as you seek His face and walk in His Grace, **you shall OVERCOME, RISE ABOVE AND GO BEYOND all the difficulties you shall face,** as you place your confidence in The Lord Jesus Christ.

<u>**THEREFORE, HAVE FAITH IN GOD!**</u>

27

"Why Is It That Believers Often Fail To Pray?"

Have you missed your time with Him? Perhaps you've neglected time with God because of doubt, too busy of a schedule, or your lack of understanding of the effects and power of prayer, both in the spiritual realm and in the physical realm of your life. God wants you to establish a **LOVE RELATIONSHIP WITH HIM,** which involves communication. He wants you to realize that when you pray, **HE WILL MOVE IN YOUR LIFE AND CIRCUMSTANCES. If you don't pray, you limit the power of God in your life.**

As we look at Biblical and secular history, there is no doubt that prayer has brought salvation to the lost, healing to the sick, strength to the weak, food to the hungry, life to the dead, deliverance to the oppressed and victory to those facing defeat. **God has a lengthy, faithful and proven history of impacting the lives of those who chose to pray.**

While prayer is one of the most talked about subjects in our churches, ministry broadcasts, and Christian circles today, **WHY IS PRAYER NOT GIVEN PRIORITY?**

Christians will talk about prayer, say that they believe in prayer, and can even explain the importance of prayer, **BUT WHY IS PRAYER SO OFTEN NEGLECTED?**

Do you know that Satan doesn't want you inspired, encouraged, strengthened, growing in faith, delivered, joyful and blessed? He knows that if he can keep you miserable, fearful, doubtful, discouraged, stressed, mad and weak, you will remain helpless, hopeless, frustrated, PRAYER-LESS, wandering aimlessly through life and even mad at God. **For the devil knows that it's in prayer that a believer will encounter and experience God.**

The devil has even convinced some of you that all the promises of God are for someone else, but not you. **But, that's a lie from the very pit of hell.**

The power of effective prayer can be seen in the lives of many throughout the pages of scripture. Through prayer, Hannah, who was childless, prayed and Samuel was born. (Read 1st Samuel, Chapter 1-2)

Through prayer, Elijah changed the weather conditions and it didn't rain for 3 ½ years in Israel. (Read 1st Kings, Chapter 17) Through prayer, Hezekiah was healed and 15 more years were added to his life. (Read 2nd Kings, Chapter 20).

The Lord Jesus Christ himself gave us many wonderful promises regarding prayer and how He would move in our lives and affairs **if** you would seek God's face and stand on His Word. (Read John 15:7)

In Luke 18:1 The Lord Jesus himself said that "Men should always pray and not faint." We clearly need to understand that in itself, prayer is not the answer. **"GOD IS!"** But, He has instructed us and still encourages believers to involve Him in every aspect of their lives by having an intimate communion with Christ through prayer.

Did you know that when you pray, God releases angels to stand right by your side? Yes, these ministering spirits are dispatched from the very throne-room of God to stand guard and protect as you're trusting Christ.

There's nothing too hard for The Lord to do, but without prevailing or effective prayer, you'll only get what life throws at you. So, why should you settle for anything less than walking in God's Spirit and experiencing His mighty hand and wonderful grace at work in your life?

Learn to put prayer first! There's nothing better than to arise early and start your day off with prayer. Learn to schedule your entire day around your communication and time of intimacy with your Heavenly Father. **He guarantees that your life will never be the same.**

Andrew Bills

28

"Are You Aware That God Does Some Of His Greatest Work In The Midst Of Your Darkest Hour?"

Darkness – To some it's their natural way of life, and to many others, they thrive by living in it. But wherever darkness is, **LIGHT always has the capacity of overpowering its control and maintaining its influence over it.** Therefore, **LIGHT** belongs in a special class of its own.

"**Light**" in the Bible is the emblem of knowledge, purity, and truth; as "**darkness**" is the emblem of ignorance, error, sin, evil, and wretchedness. Light's illuminating power and potency is only derived from The Word of God and the power of The Holy Spirit through Christ Jesus.

Genesis 1: 2-3 says, "And the earth was without form and void, and darkness was upon the face of the deep. And the Spirit of God moved upon the face of the waters. And God said, Let there be light, and there was light."

Just as you start reading the Bible, you immediately come upon this **TRUTH** starting in Genesis, where God called into existence **Light** which had no previous existence in that place. Additionally, it must be further noted that this appearance of light was not due to the mere development of nature.

From this starting scripture we learn that He not only **IS**, but that He has a commanding presence with undeniable authority and power. **"He speaks, and it is done; He commands, and it stands fast."** Light was called forth and overpowered the darkness, all from the creative mandate from God. And this was the beginning of A New Creation and this work of power and grace is exactly what's done in the heart of a person who turns to Christ today.

This **LIGHT**, which **IS CHRIST**, is still so illuminating and powerful that the message preached by the apostles was not derived from man's human reasoning, science, or from any traditions imparted from man. It was received or inspired from the very same Holy Spirit that was in the beginning.

Well, the darkness back then is the very same darkness that wants to hover over you, your family, your finances, your business or careers, and your entire lives today. But God is the God of your BREAKTHROUGH. FOR HE STILL CAN WONDERFULLY SAVE, DELIVER, HEAL, PROVIDE FOR, STRENGTHEN, BLESS, AND GRANT VICTORY in the very midst of every hard time, adverse circumstance, negative situation, painful condition, satanic entrapment, and demonic activity all through the mighty name of our Lord Jesus Christ.

You can never face, encounter, or experience any situation that can be so dark in which Christ cannot shine forth in. For **HE IS** our Bright and Morning Star, The King of Glory, The Alpha and The Omega, The First and The Last, The Beginning and The End, and **HE IS** the remedy, cure, and solution to anything that you're facing.

<u>**THEREFORE, HAVE FAITH IN GOD!**</u>

29

"Are You Allowing Someone To Talk You Out Of What God Has Revealed To You?"

During these days of satanic entrapments, false prophesying, circus antics, idiocy, insanity, and just plain lying, **you must learn and know God's Word and be led of The Holy Spirit for yourself or you'll face discouragement, defeat, and destruction.**

While I believe in the power of God and the gifts of God's Holy Spirit, have been used in these areas and have personally witnessed God moving supernaturally in these areas, **there are still those who will target and prey upon you by saying:** "God told me to tell you or I have a word from the Lord for you." And **they have not been sent by God, and you need to beware of these wolves in sheep's clothing.** God has been and forever will always be <u>**FAITHFUL TO HIS WORD**</u>, and it's there that you must always learn to trust in, rely upon, remain faithful to, and then be watchful, prayerful, and use discernment as you go forward.

In 1st Kings Chapter 13, we are given the story where God had spoken to an unnamed prophet and directed him to go prophesy against the evil king Jeroboam who had built false altars to make people worship idols all throughout the land of Judah. The anointing of God was so upon this prophet that even when Jeroboam attempted to lay his hands on this prophet, the king's hands miraculously **"dried up"** and then healed just for him to see, know, and experience God's power.

But throughout the story, we also learn that God, in his instructions to this unnamed prophet, had told him not to even eat or drink anything until he had completed his mission and had left that land after delivering the message to Jeroboam.

Unfortunately, while this unnamed prophet was faithful in delivering God's message to the evil king and he had been miraculously used by the hand of God in doing so, on his way out of that land, **he allowed Satan to distract him from God's Words to him.**

Tired from his journey, alone, wearied from the heat of the day, hungry from fasting and thirsty, as this unnamed prophet rested for a moment along the side of the road under an oak tree, an older man claiming to also be a prophet approached him with some very appealing, alluring, and persuasive words.

In 1st Kings 13:18 NIV it says, "The old prophet answered, 'I too am a prophet, as you are. And an angel said to me by the word of the LORD, 'Bring him back with you to your house so that he may eat bread and drink water.' **(But he was lying to him.)**"

A false prophet is a presenter of incorrect doctrine or one that will falsely and unjustly lay claim to divine inspiration to lead you astray. **We must remember that Satan himself can even appear as an angel of light to bring deception and ruin into our lives.**

Satan will bring suggestive thoughts into your mind or send someone directly to you saying: "It's okay, nobody will know or see you. Everybody's doing it. An angel sent me to you because you know you have needs. God told me to tell you. Or it's all right to be religious, but aren't you taking this thing too far?"

It became totally apparent that an angel of darkness and idolatry came forward to meet this unnamed prophet as an instrument to discredit God's Word, influence, then detour his mind and mission and then bring destruction into his life. The unnamed prophet arose, went back into the city with the older prophet, and dined and refreshed himself at his home, **all at the great**

displeasure of God. Then finally, on his way home out of the city, his life was shortened, as he was struck down by a ferocious lion on the main road.

Learn God's Word for yourself. Walk in obedience to Christ and then you'll experience the spiritual, supernatural hand of God moving in your life and in your affairs. Yield yourself only to The Holy Spirit's guidance. Trust in the Lord and lean not to your own understanding, but in all your ways acknowledge God and He shall direct your path.

<u>**THEREFORE, HAVE FAITH IN GOD**</u>!

30

"Why Don't You Do Something That The Enemy Doesn't Expect You To Do?"

A surprise attack before dawn on **MAY 10, 1775**, gave America one of its first victories of the Revolutionary War. **Ethan Allen, who commanded the Green Mountain Boys of Vermont, captured Fort Ticonderoga on Lake Champlain, without the loss of one man, by overrunning the British stronghold in the early morning while the British troops were sleeping.**

Rushing suddenly upon the enemy, Ethan Allen shouted: "In the Name of the Great Jehovah and the Continental Congress we demand your immediate surrender." The British surrendered and were sent back to Great Britain. Then three weeks later, in addressing the Massachusetts Congress, the joyous shout was, **"If God be for us, who can be against us?"**(Romans 8:31)

Amazing things can and will happen in our lives when we start looking to Jesus, trusting God, and rising up to go forward in faith. "The Lord is our refuge and strength, a very present help in the time of trouble." **(Psalms 46:1)**

Too often, to keep you discouraged and procrastinating, Satan sends forth "<u>the spirit of hopelessness</u>" to implant his lying thoughts to your mind to paint a vivid picture of gloom and doom before your eyes. In speaking to your mind, Satan is trying to convince you that **"there's absolutely no possible solution or any way out of your situation."**

By stealing away your hope today, Satan is trying to rob you of your future. He knows that if you're experiencing hopelessness by keeping your eyes on yourself, your feelings and your present situation, you will be distracted from following God's plan and purpose for your life. And Satan knows that you are covered by Christ's blood atonement, and does not want you to walk in the victory that is yours. He is working overtime giving you pictures of mental defeat, financial destruction, and a hopeless future. But remember he IS a defeated foe!

God wants you to realize that the only situation that's hopeless belongs to the Devil. He's the defeated one, the liar, the deceiver, the thief, the manipulator, the destroyer, and might I add, **"The loser"**!! Satan's unchangeable destiny is to be cast into The Lake of Fire! Even NOW we, as believers, are given authority over him in Jesus' name! He is UNDER our feet! **So, how can the devil really mess with your mind about your future, when Christ has already predicted and announced his?**

Remember, whenever your outlook isn't looking so good, **"Try Looking UP!"** Depression isn't a stage you go through, **"IT'S AN ATTACK!"** Discouragement and depression can lead to a physical and spiritual breakdown. It will immobilize you through frustrations and fatigue, and cause fear and bitterness. It will have draining, damaging and paralyzing effects. If you let yourself, your enthusiasm will dry up and your conversation will become sour as you become dazed and engulfed in self-pity and grief. But, The Holy Spirit of God has called you to be **"more than a conqueror"** through our Lord and Savior, Jesus Christ. **(Romans 8:37)**

Realize that you will completely surprise and anger the devil when you rise up in faith in the name of Jesus Christ and remind Satan of his place. Satan knows the power within you, but does not expect that you know it, or will use it!

NO! Satan thinks that you believe the thoughts he has implanted that tell you that you are defeated and finished. Therefore no matter how beat up or drained you might be feeling, realize that it's time for you to fight back, stand up against those negative thoughts, and rise above circumstances, by praising God. Know that you are **NOT** alone!

Stand on God's Word, get before His Presence, learn who you are in Christ, be filled with His Holy Spirit and step out in faith! Then you'll find significance and value, break the bonds of demonic influence, overcome discouragement and depression, and break free from the stress, grief, anxiety and guilt that have been holding you prisoner.

Go join that prayer group and start interceding for others. Start leaving your comfort zone, and share Christ with others in your community. Start giving with a cheerful heart to your church or ministry, and support others. Rise up and do whatever God has placed in your heart to do.

God has called you unto Himself, placed His Spirit inside of you, and now desires to work in you, through you, by you and with you.

THEREFORE, HAVE FAITH IN GOD!

Andrew Bills

31

"How To Rebound From Defeat And Start Over After Disappointments?"

My daughter was a professional basketball player for many years but one of the greatest insights that I've ever received from the Lord came at the end of one of her high school freshman games.

It had been a very tight and hard played game. The score was tied and with less than 30 seconds remaining, our team had the ball running down the court as the ball was quickly passed to her.

She quickly took aim, then the ball took its flight but the basket was missed. **Then, after much scrambling, somehow the ball found its way right back into my daughter's hands.**

Suddenly, with only a couple of seconds remaining, again she took aim. **But this time there appeared to be a difference.** Having had the bad experience of previously missing, her aim was now more carefully and skillfully planned.

She was better positioned, there was a new sparkle in her eye and a new smile on her face, she knew the score, and she was more confident as she aimed.

Then, just as the ball left her hands, the buzzer sounded and a great hush fell over the crowd as all eyes were on the ball. Suddenly, there was the sound of the ball snapping into the basket and the crowd going wild as our team began to celebrate their victory.

Just then, as people were celebrating everywhere, **The Holy Spirit spoke to my heart revealing what it takes to "<u>rebound from defeat</u>."**

Have you ever missed the mark? Have you ever tried and failed? Have you ever experienced any type of set-backs? Have you ever made any serious mistakes that you thought you'd never recover from? Do you feel confused, fractured or wounded? Have your ambitions been crushed? Do you want to be made whole?

The Holy Spirit spoke the words from Psalms 34:19 which says, "Many are the afflictions of the righteous but the Lord delivers him out of them all."

You can learn to leave your wounded past behind. You can start over after disappointments. If your dreams have been shattered, you can re-discover how to re-focus on your vision. God can bring great blessing through times of great failure, tragedy and even discouragement. You can recover loss dreams and rediscover your cutting edge.

So, open your heart to the healing touch of Jesus Christ today. **Take another look at the promises of God and re-discover His Grace and renewed hope through Jesus Christ.** Allow God's Holy Spirit to minister to your heart the words on today.

<u>THEREFORE, HAVE FAITH IN GOD!</u>

32

"Are You One Of The Lord's Heroes Of Faith?"

A hero is a person who, despite a dangerous, distressful or dismal circumstance, chooses to bravely respond or act in the midst of that dark situation. **Heroes are not perfect people, but are those who choose to rise above and look beyond the present conditions and are driven to act.**

Today, you too can be an example of one of God's heroes, by allowing your life to be characterized not by your falling down, <u>but by your rising up.</u> Many people choose to stay down when they fall, but today's heroes of faith realize that God has created them for better things, and make decisions to no longer allow their wounded pasts or hurtful present conditions keep them down or defeated.

Have you fallen? <u>**We've all failed at some point in time and learned that failure was not fatal, and refused to let it be final.**</u> But the distinction between victory and failure is in the getting back up as you allow God's promises and The Holy Spirit to seize, resurrect, ignite and strengthen your heart.

You first begin by understanding that **Proverbs 24:16 NIV says,** "For though a righteous man falls seven times, he rises again." Then secondly, you recognize that Christ daily grants mercy and grace to us. **Lamentations 3:22-24 NIV says,** "Because of the Lord's great love we are not consumed, for his compassions never fail. They are new every morning; great is your faithfulness. I say to myself, "The Lord is my portion; therefore I will wait for him."

<u>**So today, who are God's heroes of faith**</u>? They are the people that struggle to arise each morning to go to work and return

home to provide for their families. They are the drug addicts who have broken free, the teenagers who live responsibly in the face of parental alcoholism, the prostitutes who have become morally pure, the single mothers who chose not to abort, the students who chose not to drop out. These everyday heroes are the men who've chosen to be responsible role models and take care of their children, the healthy spouses that love and care for their ailing or dying spouse, and the fallen, broken and now resurrected preachers who now gratefully and mightily preach Jesus Christ.

We are the forgiven and the redeemed in Christ who are setting an example for many others to follow, knowing that the only thing that lasts forever is His Mercy and Wonderful Loving Grace.

THEREFORE, HAVE FAITH IN GOD!

33

"Do You Find Yourself Doing Things You Feel The Need To Hide?"

We've come to live in a world where anything goes. "If it feels good, do it, and let the good times roll" are continuing to be the worldly philosophies of this life. There are many who are reading steamy, alluring love books, watching X-rated movies, and are clinging onto pornographic materials that they would be highly embarrassed if discovered and too ashamed to talk about at church.

Then you've entered into darkness which violates Christian Faith principles, your spiritual code of ethics, and it can end up costing you dearly.

<u>**Is the life you're living worth the price that Christ paid upon Calvary?**</u> **Aren't we as believers instructed and encouraged to pick up our cross and follow Him daily?**

While there are those who actually think, believe, or act as if The Lord can't see their sin if they try and hide it under a cloak of darkness or perform it in a locked room, **but can any of your activities be concealed from His all-seeing eye? Can anyone entertain displeasing thoughts and believe that He won't know the intentions of your heart?**

1st **John 1:6 NIV says,** "If we claim to have fellowship with him and yet walk in the darkness, we lie and do not live out the truth."

The Apostle John, under the anointing of The Holy Spirit of God, says if you're walking, living, and continually practicing sin, then you're living a lie and walking in error.

The leading thought is that if you live in sin, it's evidence and proof that your life is a contradiction, denoting that you're ignorant of the righteousness of Christ, walking in blindness and unbelief, and therefore a stranger to The Spirit of God.

Then this makes a person who lives in habitual sin a false professor, a pretender, one living in deception, and it's hard to believe that such a person could be a Christian.

How can a person who is not a partaker of God's divine nature ever believe that they are going to heaven? How can a person participate in some Christian rites without ever receiving the love of Christ in their heart, without knowing the peace of God in their mind and the joy of The Holy Spirit in their life?

Eternal life through Jesus Christ means to have been washed from our sins in His blood. And in this dark world, we who have been redeemed by the blood of Christ and are led by the Spirit of God, **must know that we are representing the nature of God and His Word through our ongoing lifestyle.**

If you try to hide yourself or attempt to cover up or keep secret your activities, **the devil will additionally expose you to further ruin your character, credibility, respectability, and relationships. <u>No attempt to disguise yourself will profit.</u>** And there's no art of concealment that you can entertain or conduct that will hide you from God or prevent you from reaping what you've sown.

It costs something to miss out on all the so-called fun that everyone in the world is having. **But it costs something to make the decision not to walk with the world and live for Christ.** And the rewards for following Christ and living a Godly lifestyle are simply and eternally wonderful.

<u>**THEREFORE, HAVE FAITH IN GOD!**</u>

34

"Is Seeing Really Believing?"

The Bible says that we walk by faith, not by sight. Without faith, the Bible says, that it's impossible to please God. So, why do people naturally take on the attitude that **"Doubting Thomas"** had in the Bible?

In John 20:24-29 we are given intriguing the story of doubting Thomas. John 20:25 declares, "So the other disciples told him, "We have seen the Lord!" But he said to them, "Unless I see the nail marks in his hands and put my finger where the nails were, and put my hand into his side, I will not believe it."

Due to his broken heart, deep grief and crushed spirit, Thomas absolutely refused to believe the mere testimony of the other disciples. He required proof in order to be satisfied. His sin of unbelief was more aggravated because he was present at the raising of Lazarus from the dead by Jesus and had heard Christ himself say, that he should rise from the dead the third day.

Now after rejecting the proof from the other disciples, Thomas could have remained in his state of unbelief, **but Christ chose to reveal Himself to Thomas for examination to touch his heart and impact his life.** Then Jesus approved the faith of Thomas, but more highly commends the faith of those who should believe without having ever visibly seen Him.

And just like Thomas, God loves you and longs to have a personal relationship with you. He wants to show you how to walk by faith and lead a fulfilled life. **As we spend time with him and grow in our relationship with him, he will impart spiritual truths to us through His Word and Holy Spirit.**

Now, in many ways we act just like Thomas, when our confidence or strength is based on seeing, touching, hearing, tasting and feeling. Somehow we trust our senses more than God and His Promises and respond more confidently to the things we see in the present than to the unseen and eternal things of God. So when you put your confidence in such things, you WILL be disappointed.

How can you trust in anything if the things and people you see, relate to and put your trust in are unreliable and on shaky ground?

There is often deception when we depend on our feelings, circumstances, and our immediate surroundings. They can lead us to think things are hopeless, and that what we see is all that there is. **But God's laws are both spiritual and universal principles of faith.** And that the exercising of your faith is always well pleasing to Christ and God always blesses those that trust in and rely on His Word.

This brief passage of scripture reveals that we can always trust The Lord to keep His promise even when we can't see, hear, or touch him in the natural. **He is faithful and will always be constant and consistent to His Eternal Word.**

35

"When The Thief Comes, Will He Find You Armed & Dangerous?"

In these days of terrorist, senseless, cowardly, demonic, and organized antichrist attacks from evil and soul-less individuals or groups, you must become prepared for the battle. But first realize that your security and strength will not come in the form of new gun control laws or legislation, **but in the power of God.**

Jesus has alerted us that a sinister killer is on the prowl behind the scenes and is going for the jugular vein to deliver knockout blows from which he doesn't want you to ever recover from. And usually this battlefield location first is an unprecedented attack starting in the mind.

In John 10:10, Jesus said that "The thief (the devil) comes to steal, kill, and to destroy, but **I AM** come that you might have Life, and that they might have it more abundantly."

Now, while the devil's diabolical devices or schemes are not new today, his ungodly strategy is to choke out the 3 abiding essentials in the life of every believer, which are **Faith, Hope, and Love. And you need all 3 of these to survive and press on through the storms of life towards victory in Christ.**

First, Satan attacks Faith by attempting to make you **skeptical**. Then he attacks hope by working to make you **cynical**. Finally, he attacks love by trying to make you **critical**. Satan's most used tools for attacking our minds are: **Delays, Distractions, and Discouragements.** So whenever you're being bombarded and overwhelmed by any of these diabolical devices, you can find comfort and strength by standing on God's Living Word, in the power of His Holy Spirit, and through creating an atmosphere of glorious praise.

Despite sickness, financial hard times, abusiveness, family division, or any other type of spiritual warfare, when Satan begins to move in for the kill, **don't be too quick to wave a white flag of surrender because God is still a very present help in the times of struggle and need.**

As a believer you must realize that you are the most vulnerable or susceptible whenever you are discouraged. <u>So, do you know who your antidote is?</u>

<u>Jesus Christ</u>! You must get back into His presence and learn how to encourage yourself in The Lord. Begin to shore up your faith in God's Word and then allow The Holy Spirit to uncap new reservoirs within you.

Then, according to Ephesians Chapter 6, put on the whole armor of God and rise up to start living again. Step out in the authority of Jesus Christ and work to restrain or prevent evil from claiming supremacy over your life. **Show proof that His love and grace still abides today and that you will not take down or be overcome, but will continue to stand in Christ Jesus.**

Romans 12:21 says, "Do not be overcome by evil, but overcome evil with good." We must not allow ourselves to become vanquished, subdued, or defeated by the actions of any evil, unbalanced, drug-addicted, confused, or rebellious person.

As we continue to stand against all evil activity and opposition in our society and world, we must not step down to the level of any ungodly circumstance, abandon our principles of faith or Christian values, nullify our prayers or forget about God's future judgment and His Eternal Plan.

<u>**THEREFORE, HAVE FAITH IN GOD!**</u>

36

"You Don't Drown By Falling Into The Water, You Drown By Staying There"

It has been said that "You don't drown by falling into the water, you drown by staying there." **Therefore, God can use whatever you've experienced to be a blessing many others as you trust Him to take you through your circumstance.**

Learning to trust Jesus Christ to bring something good out of a painful situation or an unexpected tragedy means **looking beyond what we can see** as you surrender to God.

Our Lord Jesus Christ is in the business of turning your mess into a wonderful message, your liability into an asset and your painful experience into an insightful blessing to encourage the lives of countless others. **For up from the ashes,** God always brings forth those soldiers or warriors that cling to His Word as their only hope for survival as they go through an emotional ordeal or anguish during their painful circumstance.

"No matter what you're going through, Jesus Has Already Worked It Out For You," are the faithful words we share at the conclusion of our daily broadcasts. We believe and teach that there's nothing Greater Than God that you can experience or that God can't use for good, if you place it into His hands.

Such was the case in 2010 as my wife, Ann Marie was diagnosed with a very rare tumor lodged in her neck that paralyzed her left vocal cord, affected the hearing in her left ear, stopped her ability to sing and left her only with a speaking voice at the level of a whisper.

God had blessed her with a beautiful singing voice, one of which many had told her she sang like an angel. Now she had to determine how to face this dilemma after having used her beautiful gift for over 36 years. Throughout this ordeal, Ann Marie experienced great frustration and sadness until she decided she would not allow her voice to define her. As she opened her Bible, **she received great inspiration from John 1:4 NIV which says,** "And light shined in the darkness, but darkness could not overcome it."

What a simple and yet profound revelation this was to her. **That Light could not be overcome by darkness,** for darkness represented the tumor in her head, the sadness of losing her voice, inner anguish and the value of who she was and what she thought she had to share.

She had read that portion of scripture many, many times before but this time it was different as The Holy Spirit of God gave her a new revelation and understanding from God's Word.

The laser surgery went well but the surgeon told me not to get my hopes up for the restoration of her voice. I told him, **"Doctor, you're a good physician but I know the Great Physician and we're standing on His Word for her full recovery."**

Upon the 3rd anniversary of her surgery, after only being able to talk above a whisper throughout that time, her full speaking ability has returned. Many have heard Ann Marie faithfully speaking and teaching over the internet radio broadcasts sitting right by my side sharing out of her heart. Each week she conducts and teaches the Women's Bible Study sessions. Her singing capability, which is about 80 percent restored, is still briefly limited and keeping her from hitting the high beautiful notes but is still a work in progress as we're looking to Christ.

But her greatest blessing is in what Christ has done inside of her. She's received a greater revelation of His Love and Grace and that her true calling was to serve Christ through encouraging others in His Word. And through this entire ordeal, she's now touching more lives for Christ.

My friends, only God can make sense out of nonsense as you trust Him. There's nothing too hard for Him to do. He specializes in the most difficult and impossible situations.

His only question to you is: **"Will you trust Me even if you don't understand or can't see what I'm trying to do in your life?"**

Andrew Bills

37

"Have You Experienced The Power And Healing Of Forgiveness Through Christ?"

In these days of broken marriages, divided homes, abusiveness, humiliation, abandonment, deception, stressful living and frivolous law suits, **God is declaring that your very first step towards recovery and inner healing lies in forgiveness.**

Referred to as ambassador of the power of forgiveness in Christ, Cornelia "Corrie" ten Boom earlier had been sent to a concentration camp and was imprisoned, along with her father and other family members, during World War II. Under the horrendous conditions in Nazi Germany, she saw all of them die at the hands of their Nazi abusers.

"God does not have problems, only plans," she later proclaimed after learning that a clerical error allowed her to be released from that Nazi concentration camp only one week before all the women prisoners her age were executed.

Though she was released from the horror of Ravensbruck concentration camp, Corrie continued to live with a remarkable reliance on God, just as her family earlier had as they hid Jews in the Dutch Underground, during the Nazi invasion of The Netherlands, during the Holocaust.

But, while she was miraculously able to live through such horror, **her supreme test came when she later came face to face again with one of the perpetrators.** While she was teaching in Germany in 1947, she was approached by a former Ravensbrück camp guard, who had been known as one of the cruelest guards.

At first, she was very reluctant to forgive him, but prayed that she would be able to as they stood face to face grasping each other's hands. **Her flesh was reminding her that he was a former cruel Nazi guard and that she was the former prisoner who had suffered such cruelty and had lost everything.** She later said that she had never known God's love as intensely as she did at that very moment.

She also wrote that in her post-war experience with other victims of Nazi brutality, **only those who were able to forgive were able to rebuild their lives.**

In The Lord's Prayer, in Matthew 6:14 NIV Jesus said, "For if you forgive other people when they sin against you, your heavenly Father will also forgive you." Too many people have made themselves subject to revenge, but he who shows mercy shall experience greater mercy and the grace of God.

So forgiveness allows you to let go of past events, be healed and then move on with your life. **Forgiveness destroys the ability of others to hold you as a "prisoner."** When you forgive others, you're declaring that you will no longer be **"victimized"** by people or past circumstances, **as you're proclaiming that Christ is now the focus of your new life and walk.** Forgiveness means that you're laying it all at the foot of the cross and surrendering it all to Christ.

Forgiveness doesn't mean that we're denying the existence of any type of disappointment, rejection, ridicule, betrayal, deception, hurt or any abusive situation. **NO!** It means that you're taking authority over your circumstances through your new life in Jesus Christ and that you're **NOT** going to permit or allow any **"old carnal fleshly feelings"** to no longer reign over, control, hinder or destroy your life.

The key towards preventing or stopping pain in our lives starts with forgiveness. It is the first step towards you having or receiving total recovery. Forgiveness is not a onetime singular act; it's an ongoing demonstration of maturity through The Holy Spirit of God and His Word. And remember that as Christ forgives you of your sins, you must forgive those who trespassed against you.

38

"Are You Tuned In To The Voice Of The Holy Spirit?"

The true story happened back when the telegraph was the fastest method of long distance communication, as a young man applied for a job as a Morse code operator.

Answering an ad in the newspaper, he went to the office address that was listed. When he arrived, he entered a large, busy office filled with noise and clatter, including the sound of the telegraph in the background. **A sign on the receptionist's counter instructed job applicants to fill out a form and wait until they were summoned to enter the inner office.**

The young man filled out his form and sat down with the seven other applicants in the waiting area. **After a few minutes, the young man stood up, crossed the room to the door of the inner office, and walked right in.**

Naturally the other applicants perked up, wondering what was going on. They muttered among themselves that they hadn't heard any summons yet. They assumed that the young man who went into the office made a mistake and would be disqualified.

Within a few minutes, however, the employer escorted the young man out of the office and said to the other applicants, **"Gentlemen, thank you very much for coming, but the job has just been filled."**

The other applicants began grumbling to each other, and one spoke up saying, **"Wait a minute, I don't understand. He was the last to come in, and we never even got a chance to be interviewed. Yet he got the job. That's not fair!"**

The employer said, "I'm sorry, but all the time you've been sitting here, the telegraph has been ticking out the following message in Morse code: '**If you understand this message, then come right in. The job is yours.**' None of you heard it or understood it. This young man did. The job is his.

Are your ears tuned in to The Voice Of The Holy Spirit? The Lord speaks through the Bible, The Holy Spirit and even to us through our circumstances, but **are you listening to what He's saying?**

Many today have pre-determined in their minds what they want to hear, follow or ignore through the process of **"selective hearing"** when it comes to listening and obeying The Lord.

While recognizing His Voice is just the beginning, walking in obedience is what's difficult and hinders many people. **In John 10:27 Jesus said** "My sheep listen to my voice; I know them, and they follow me."

Those willing to follow Christ **must yield themselves to his guidance, seek to be led and directed by Him as you tune in to The Voice of The Holy Spirit of God.**

Is there anything that's hindering you from hearing and obeying the voice of The Holy Spirit of God? If so, then ask yourself, **"Is anything really worth missing God?"**

39

"How To Tell If You're Moved More By What You Physically See Or If You're Moved By Christ And The Power of God"

A Sunday School Teacher walked her class out of the church building into the yard and suddenly pointed directly to the sun. **Then she said,** "While the sun is about 108 times larger than the earth, you can block out your view of the sun with any small object in your hand by simply holding it up between you and your view of the sun."

Just like in that illustration, **you too will lose your perspective when you stare at the problem directly in front of your eyes** and begin to lose sight of the greatness and glory of God.

Suddenly, you've just allowed your problem to blind you and convince you that it's bigger and greater than The Lord. Then fear will begin to creep in and rise up and you'll begin to lose perspective.

Such was the case in the book of Numbers chapter 13. Moses sent 12 men to search out and spy in the land of Canaan, then to return back with a report of what they saw.

At the end of 40 days, they returned bringing evidence of good fruit, but 10 of the spies brought forth a negative report and stirred up all of Israel with words of fear and unbelief. Only Joshua and Caleb stood alongside of Moses by faith.

Numbers 13: 30-33 NIV says, "Then Caleb silenced the people before Moses and said, 'We should go up and take possession of the land, for we can certainly do it.' But the men who had gone up with him said, 'We can't attack those people; they are stronger than we are.' And they spread among the Israelites a bad report about the land they had explored. They said, 'The land we explored devours those living in it. All the people we saw there are of great size. We saw the giants, the descendants of Anak, which were from the giants, we seemed like grasshoppers in our own eyes, and we looked the same to them.'"

Because of Israel's unbelief in The God who had divinely and mightily brought great deliverance and performed miracles in their lives, they ended up spending 40 years in that terrible wilderness, which originally would have only taken them 11 days to complete that journey if they would have continued in faith.

Now, what are the spiritual similarities or Christian lessons that we can learn from this particular experience?

If I could sum it all up in one singular sentence: **"The Lord wants our lives to be governed by obedience in faith to His Word and to rely on the power of His Holy Spirit."** We too must remember that unbelief offends and angers God. So, don't doubt in your heart and allow unbelief to shut you out from God's greatest blessings.

Unbelief reduces, limits, or restricts your options only to what you physically see or intellectually sense. Faith in God refuses to be held captive to all of those boundaries, barriers, and hindrances and always sees an open door or **"a way out of no way"** through Christ Jesus.

So, are you moved more by what you physically see or are you moved by Christ and The Power of God?

Can you see through or beyond your immediate difficult circumstances or are you being held prisoner by doubt and unbelief? Placing your confidence in the Almighty, Invisible, Awesome, and Supernatural Resurrected and Living Christ will continue to renew and reinforce your faith in all the areas in front of you.

So, don't tell God how big your mountain in front of your eyes is. **Start telling your mountains how big your God is!** As you stand on His Word and allow Him to reign in your life and orchestrate in your affairs, you too will realize that "There's nothing too hard for God to do."

Andrew Bills

40

"Show The Devil That You Don't Believe You're Defeated"

Are you counting on God for your breakthrough and victory? The Cross and The Resurrection of Christ is our assurance that God has given us the victory over all of our enemies in every conflict that we face, in the mighty name of Jesus Christ.

Today, many people are now facing some of the most horrific situations that they've ever encountered before. Lives are being destroyed by drug addiction or chemical dependency. Financial hardship is crushing homes, abusiveness is crippling lives and time won't permit me here to list all of the other demonic activities or satanic entrapments that are wreaking havoc throughout our cities today.

As the powers of darkness are opposing you, **wishful thinking or mere hoping will not resolve your dilemma or cure your situation.** Trying to handle matters on your very own really won't work out well for you either. **Only the power and authority of God's Word through faith in Jesus Christ will.**

One has only to pick up the Bible and start reading from the beginning to discover God's Eternal Existence, His Supremacy, His Authority, His Power and His Grace.

Well, Don't You Know That You Completely Surprise The Devil When You Rise Up In His Face In Faith, In The Name Of Jesus Christ, And Stand On God's Word?

The powers of darkness never expect you to do that. Satan though you were defeated! **NO!!!** More so, he thought you **even thought that you were defeated** and finished. So stand up and show the devil that you don't believe that you're defeated by glorifying Christ and going forward.

Publicly declare that the crisis you're experiencing will **NOT** take you down, out or under **and it's just another opportunity for you to encounter the grace and power of The Lord Jesus Christ.** Then start celebrating and glorifying Christ for your breakthrough the moment you turn things over to The Lord.

Remember the true and precious words in a song which said, **"Don't wait till the battle is over, shout now. For you know in the end we're going to win!"**

Celebrating is a great part of victory. Celebrate with those who may have helped, assisted, aided, showed kindness or been involved with you throughout your situation. But don't be surprised after its all over how many others will show up to claim to have been one in spirit with you all along.

We too must learn what David discovered, that God Almighty is **"The Lord Of The Breakthrough."**

In **2nd Samuel chapter 5,** once again we read of the enemy forces attacking David and the nation of Israel. But, we also read about God's supernatural divine intervention in their midst.

2nd Samuel 5:20 NLT says, "So David went to Baal-perazim and defeated the Philistines there. "The LORD did it!" David exclaimed. "He burst through my enemies like a raging flood!" So he named that place Baal-perazim (which means "the Lord who bursts through").

As a soldier who placed his confidence in God, David asked for a plan of attack from God, who was his real commander-in-chief. God so mightily moved, David declared **it was like water bursting through the wall of a dam** which quickly brought destruction to everything that was in its way.

By acting in perfect obedience, David succeeded where King Saul had failed and totally defeated the Philistines. **Obedience** to God's instructions or Word was David's key to experiencing the miraculous intervention of God.

Obedience and Praise are THE KEYS TO YOUR BREAKTHROUGH. Make a conscious decision to spend time with God in daily fellowship and praise. Then you'll be able to see the mighty hand of God move in your midst.

While salvation is free, it didn't come cheap! It cost God the very best He had to offer, **HIS SON!** Now, Christ is able to bring salvation, deliverance and grace right into your midst, **but give Him your undivided attention.** In doing so you're showing the devil that you're **Not** defeated and that you're trusting Jesus and moving forward.

Romans 8:31 NIV then says, "What, then, shall we say in response to these things? If God is for us, who can be against us?

If The Holy Spirit of God is engaged to bring us through, which of our enemies can withstand His awesome Word and mighty outstretched hand? **NONE CAN!!!**

Therefore since He has promised to
"Never leave you or forsake you."
Will you speak these same words to Him?

About The Author

MISTAKES!!! Life doesn't come without having made some, and I've made my share of them which have greatly affected my life.

But by the Grace of God, they didn't cost my life.

Now it's out of both my learned experiences and my fellowship with The Lord, as I firmly stand on God's Word in faith, that I preach and offer these inspired and prophetic messages of Salvation, Grace, Deliverance, Healing, Power, **and Victory through Jesus Christ.**

Since I've faced some of the most **"incredible impossibilities"** a person could ever face, my purpose is to help you understand God's Love, Mercy, Forgiveness, Strength and Power in the face of adverse circumstances, negative situations, painful conditions, and satanic entrapments that threaten your life, home, and family.

You Too Can Be Victorious Through Faith In Jesus Christ!

While **Andrew Bills** is a loving husband, father and grandfather, he has preached in various churches including Baptists, Pentecostal, Charismatic Catholic, and Non-Denominational Faith Ministries, despite any minor doctrinal differences, he continues to reach out and touch lives in today's world with the very inspiring and special message of **"Victory Thru Calvary."**

He's been in ministry for over 30 years, has a Bachelor's Degree and has served in many different capacities including Pastor, Lecturer, Advisor, Broadcaster, Author, Evangelist and in various managerial positions throughout the Logistics & Warehousing Industry.

As a preacher of Jesus Christ and as a teacher to the Body of Christ, he's influenced many as he continues to build Faith, brings Hope, Joy, Inspiration, and Deliverance to many hungry souls.

Books By Andrew Bills

Increase your library with these life-changing, scriptural, practical, powerful and victorious readable books of faith and wisdom from The Holy Spirit of God.

Up From The Ashes

There's No Such Thing As A Hopeless Situation

Never Step Down To The Level Of Your Circumstances

How Long Should You Wait For Your Prayers To Be Answered?

How To Crush The Works Of The Enemy Over Your Life

Will You Trust Me Even If You Don't Understand Or Can't See What I'm Doing?

Having Faith That God Can See

How To Overcome Your Wounded Past

Ministry Contact Information:

Andrew Bills Ministries Inc.
"The Victory Report Hour"
PO Box 6811, Orange, CA 92863

Website Address:
www.andrewbills.com

Email Address:
andrewbillsministries@yahoo.com

www.ingramcontent.com/pod-product-compliance
Lightning Source LLC
LaVergne TN
LVHW051131080426
835510LV00018B/2344